PLAIN
TALK
ON
Colossians

PLAIN TALK ON
Colossians

MANFORD GEORGE GUTZKE
PH.D.

**Lamplighter
Books** Grand Rapids,
Michigan
Zondervan Publishing House

PLAIN TALK ON COLOSSIANS
Copyright © 1981 by The Zondervan Corporation
Grand Rapids, Michigan

Lamplighter Books are published by Zondervan
Publishing House, 1415 Lake Drive, S.E.,
Grand Rapids, Michigan 49506

Edited by Phyllis Robinson

Library of Congress Cataloging in Publication Data

Gutzke, Manford George.
    Plain talk on Colossians.

    1. Bible.   N.T.   Colossians—Commentaries.
I. Title.

ISBN 0-310-41961-1

Printed in the United States of America

85 86 87 88 — 10 9 8 7 6 5 4 3

CHAPTER 1

† † †

SALUTATION
(Colossians 1:1–2)

Can you see why it is important for us to know who wrote this message and to whom it is addressed?

> Paul, an apostle of Jesus Christ by the will of God, and Timothy our brother, to the saints and faithful brethren in Christ which are at Colossae: Grace be unto you, and peace, from God our Father and the Lord Jesus Christ (Col. 1:1–2).

These are the opening words in the book of Colossians. It will be good for us to begin by reminding ourselves of the significance of the New Testament epistles. If you are acquainted with Bible language, you will know that we speak of the *book* of Deuteronomy or the *book* of 1 Kings. Sometimes we talk about reading the prophecy of Amos or Jeremiah, but generally speaking we call the Old Testament books just by the term *books*. When we come to the New Testament, we remember the first four books—Matthew, Mark, Luke, and John—are called the Gospels. The book of Acts is a book of history, although we do not always designate it that way. Beginning with Romans, we refer to them as epistles.

The word "epistle" means a letter, so the epistles refer to the letters that were written by the apostles to believing people. The book of Colossians, for example, is actually a letter written by an apostle of Jesus Christ; namely, the apostle Paul. And we can expect this letter to be a message from the Lord who is writing through His apostle to the believers who are gathered together in that particular city. You will notice that this letter does not try to persuade people to be saved, because the people to whom it is written are already saved. They belong to the Lord. This book is not written to

careless people to make them careful nor is it written to indifferent people to make them thoughtful. Indifferent and
careless people will not read it. It is written to guide interested, earnest people in the direction they should go. Even
after you have accepted the Lord Jesus Christ as your Savior,
you will still need to learn how to walk with Him.

For example, when a young woman has married the man
she loves, she will now be eager to find out what she should
do to please her husband. In a similar manner, after you have
accepted the Lord Jesus Christ as your Savior, you really want
to please Him. That needs to be learned. It is important to
remember that the believer is motivated by his love for
Christ. Our love for Christ is in response to His love for us.
The love that prompted Him to come and die for us will
prompt us to want to live for Him. "The love of Christ con-
straineth us" (2 Cor. 5:14), and even if we are weak we have
an inward urgency to want to be well pleasing in His sight.

Maybe you are living in a situation where you can make
very little change. Perhaps you are in a practical situation,
working in an office, where you do not have the opportunity
to make changes. But you can share in the situation and while
you are working in that office, going to that school, or living in
that home, you can so conduct yourself that you witness to the
name of the Lord Jesus Christ. And you can witness better
and share more when you know what you should do. This is
what Paul undertakes to develop and to promote when he
writes. He writes to strengthen believers in Christ so that
they may be strong in faith, giving glory to God.

Now let us look at the salutation in the opening of this
epistle. Almost all of Paul's letters start out with his own name
and then a personal word: "I, myself, an apostle of Jesus
Christ by the will of God." When Paul called himself an
apostle of Jesus Christ he meant that he was an authorized,
commissioned representative of Jesus Christ. "By the will of
God." He was given this commission, not by the will of man
and not by his own will. "To the saints and faithful brethren in
Christ which are at Colossae." The word "saints" refers to
believers who have been sanctified by the will of God. The
word "sanctified" means set apart for God by the will of God.
They are saints in the sense that they are chosen and sepa-

rated from; the way in which, when a woman becomes a wife, she is chosen from and separated from other women. So believers personally belong to the Lord.

"And faithful brethren in Christ." Now this word "faithful" does not refer to the quality of their integrity or their steadfastness, but it refers to their actual experience as "believing" brethren in Christ. They were brethren because they believed in Christ. This was not a tribute to their persistence but to their action. They were "faithful" in the sense that they believed. This refers to believing souls who have accepted Christ and are now united to Him by faith, having been adopted as children of God and receiving the Holy Spirit. These are brethren in Christ.

"Grace and peace." Grace is the divine enablement to do God's will, and peace is the consequence of obeying Him.

THE BELIEVER'S EXPERIENCE
(Colossians 1:3–5)

Have you ever fully realized what it means to a believer in Christ to be with other believers?

> We give thanks to God and the Father of our Lord Jesus Christ, praying always for you, since we heard of your faith in Christ Jesus, and of the love which ye have to all the saints, for the hope which is laid up for you in heaven, whereof ye heard before in the word of the truth of the gospel (Col. 1:3–5).

This passage emphasizes that the apostle Paul was thankful for other believers, and in these words he shows his normal attitude toward them. I urge you in your personal devotions to thank God for the believers you know and for their faith. Thank God they are not indifferent people, that they really care for you and for the things of the gospel. We need to keep in mind that people are not naturally believers in Christ. Some people are better behaved than others, but I am talking about being a believer in Christ.

One does not become a believer in Christ simply by getting to be older. You become a believer by receiving Jesus Christ as your Savior. Whosoever will may become a believer in Christ through faith, but faith in itself is a gift of God. Many intelligent people have approached the matter of receiving Christ from a human point of view. They have applied their minds and their intentions to this. They have studied the Bible, human psychology, and the testimonies of people who have tried to become believers in Christ, yet they are still in the dark. They have never met the Lord because they have never looked for Him. Salvation becomes a matter of our receiving Him who came for us. As we receive Him, we become the children of God. God regenerates us. We are born again. If Christ had not come—if Christ had not died and been raised from the dead, if Christ had not been taken into the presence of God and exalted at the right hand of God—there would be no such thing as the Christian experience. And so Paul thanks God, who has called these people into faith.

Now the believer's experience is reflected in these verses and we see here a classic description of it. The believer's experience develops in three major ways or perspectives. These are indicated by the words "faith," "hope," and "love."

Notice the first one, faith in Christ Jesus. The apostle says "We give thanks to God . . . praying always for you . . . since we heard of your faith in Christ Jesus." Faith in Christ Jesus means much more than just knowledge about Him. Pilate knew that Christ lived but he was not a believer; Judas and Satan also knew of His existence but did not have saving faith. Saving faith is a case of believing that Christ Jesus died for our sins, He was buried, He was raised in the newness of life for us, and He is now in the presence of God with joy. Faith in Him accepts all this. When I believe in Jesus Christ I accept that He died for my sins: that is what I accept for my ego. Christ was buried: that guides me in my self-denial. He was raised in the newness of life: that provides for my new nature. Just as He did all these things with joy, so I receive all these things with thanks. In this active committal of self into the hands of the living Lord, I receive these things which make way for the second perspective: "the love which ye have to all the saints."

This word "love" does not mean sentiment. It is a word that indicates interest in the welfare and happiness of others. Love might be seen in being charitable to the poor, and in many other ways. This "love to all the saints" is a feeling that you have for other believers in which you wish them well. Love is not operative because they are special friends of yours, or because they are economically on your level. The believer in Christ has an accepting attitude toward all believers.

In the practice of such active goodwill to all others, the believer in Christ may suffer loss. But all this is more than compensated for by the last of the three perspectives: "for the hope which is laid up for you in heaven." The phrase here "in heaven" is not necessarily after your body has been put in the grave. Heaven is right now, but it is different from this world. This world means the earth, and heaven is where God is. Heaven is real, but it is spiritual; it is not the same as this world. This needs to be understood and it is understood in the revelation of the gospel. This is why Paul says, "Whereof ye heard before in the word of the truth of the gospel." Gospel preaching by the apostles sets forth the spiritual values that are available now. They are for us right now in heaven, which is where God is.

THE GOSPEL AT WORK
(Colossians 1:6–8)

Do you realize that every believer in Christ is a member of God's family because he responded to the gospel?

> Which is come unto you, as it is in all the world; and bringeth forth fruit, as it doth also in you, since the day ye heard of it, and knew the grace of God in truth: as ye also learned of Epaphras our dear fellow servant, who is for you a faithful minister of Christ; who also declared unto us your love in the Spirit (Col. 1:6–8).

In these words we learn something about the gospel, and then something about believers in Christ. What Paul says about the gospel is that it is preached to all men offering salvation through Christ Jesus. The preaching of the gospel brings forth fruit; and the fruit that it brings forth is the faith of the believers. This gospel is the same as that expressed by the apostle Paul when he wrote to the Corinthian believers (1 Cor. 15:8). The gospel, as it is set forth there, is that Christ

Jesus came into the world to save sinners, He died for sinners, He was buried, He rose again from the dead for the believer, and He was seen after His resurrection. These are certain facts about Jesus Christ in His earthly life, with an interpretation of those facts. The record indicated that the Colossian believers heard the gospel. So they knew the grace of God in truth, and that is what made it operative in them.

How does the gospel work in our hearts? We need to hear the gospel preached, then we need to believe it. The word "hearing" means much more than that the utterance is heard. It means that it is heard with understanding. The narrated facts of Jesus Christ were what these people heard when the gospel was preached, so they knew the grace of God in truth. The grace of God that they knew was what God does for human beings who believe. God did this in Christ Jesus, and so we say in the benediction, "The grace of the Lord Jesus Christ be with you all." The grace of God was to send Jesus Christ into this world for men who did not deserve Him so that we might receive freely eternal life from God.

The facts of the incarnation of Jesus Christ must not only be stated but must be interpreted for an understanding of the promises. This leads believers today to understand that communicating the gospel—preaching it, teaching it, telling it to children—means telling the events. Telling the gospel of the Lord Jesus Christ means telling human beings that "God sent His Son into the world to die. God raised His Son from the dead. God took His Son to be with Him in heaven. He sent the Holy Spirit into the hearts of those who believe." This truth must be explained to people. This includes telling the events and showing the promise in them by the grace of God. The promise is that as Christ Jesus died on Calvary's cross believers by faith can reckon themselves to be crucified with Him. Since Christ was raised from the dead, they can believe that as Christ was raised, they can be regenerated. As Christ was taken into the presence of God, so they can live in the presence of God constantly. As God sent His Holy Spirit into the hearts of believers, believers today can receive the Holy Spirit into their hearts.

This kind of interpretation helps believers to understand and to believe what was done for them in Christ Jesus.

As ye also learned of Epaphras our dear fellow servant, who is
for you a faithful minister of Christ (Col. 1:7).

This truth can be confirmed to believers, and they can be
helped to understand it through other believers. This interpretation of the gospel had been preached by Epaphras
"our dear fellow servant, who is for you a faithful minister of
Christ." Paul said two things about Epaphras: he was a dear
fellow servant and he was a faithful minister of Christ. The
word "faithful" means not only that he persisted but also that
Epaphras was a man who exercised his faith. He preached the
gospel, knowing that the people who heard it could believe,
receive, and be saved. The Colossians came to know Christ
better through the ministry of Epaphras.

Who also declared unto us your love in the Spirit (Col. 1:8).

Epaphras reported to Paul the love these people had. Paul
was the former pastor of this church, so Epaphras reported to
a former pastor how the Colossians took care of and respected
him. He described how they treated him in the Spirit, as they
were guided by the Lord Jesus Christ Himself.

THE WAY TO PRAY
(Colossians 1:9–11)

Isn't it true that many times believers pray selfishly?

For this cause we also, since the day we heard it, do not cease
to pray for you, and to desire that ye might be filled with the
knowledge of his will in all wisdom and spiritual understanding; that ye might walk worthy of the Lord unto all pleasing,
being fruitful in every good work, and increasing in the knowledge of God; strengthened with all might, according to his
glorious power, unto all patience and long-suffering with joyfulness (Col. 1:9–11).

I wonder what James meant when he wrote, "Ye have not
because ye ask not," and when he said, "Ye ask, and receive
not, because ye ask amiss"?
Some years ago when I was a pastor in Dallas, I received a
phone call to come to a hospital to see someone I did not
know. The woman wanted a pastor to pray for her husband

who was seriously ill. I went and learned that the man was near death. The wife eagerly asked me to pray for her husband, which I did. I asked that he be given grace, and that the Lord might help him in the hours of weakness. I prayed that the Lord would see him through safely to Himself. When we left the room the woman turned on me in a fury because I did not pray that he would get well. I tried to reason with her and have often thought since how many people, when they turn to prayer, want only one particular thing, and nothing else.

Notice closely how the apostle Paul prays for the Colossians. "For this cause we also" (you will find the cause in vv. 10, 11, and 12) "since the day we heard it" (look at vv. 6, 7, and 8) "do not cease to pray for you." Not once for all, but over and over, praying. "And to desire" (and here we have the prayer) "that ye might be filled with the knowledge of his will in all wisdom and spiritual understanding." What would be the knowledge of His will? Since they had just become believers in Christ, Paul prayed that they might realize what this really meant. The will of God does not refer to what is going to happen tomorrow morning, or what is going to happen in business ventures or to crops. What God is seeking to produce in the believer is that he might be filled with an understanding and realization of what it means to have Christ in him. "In all wisdom": (whenever the word "wisdom" is used it means just good common sense) ". . . and spiritual understanding."

It is most important that new believers fully understand what God plans for the life of every believer. God plans that Christ Jesus shall live His life in them. This is most important for them to grasp. Here is something that could slip by easily, so let us look at it again. "Pray for you, and to desire that ye might be filled with the knowledge of his will" with an understanding of what it really means to be a believer in Christ; what it means to have Christ in the heart. "In all wisdom and spiritual understanding": with spiritual insight so that the believer may really know what it means to have Christ in him always, the hope of glory. In verses 10 and 11 we learn why this is so important. This makes it possible that "ye might walk worthy of the Lord unto all pleasing." It is the way the believer actually lives that can make him worthy of the indwelling Christ.

"Being fruitful in every good work." The believer will be found strong and fruitful, in every good work if he has Christ in him, and is "increasing in the knowledge of God." The more he walks with Christ and works with Him, the more he will know God. This knowledge will grow in him. "Strengthened with all might, according to his glorious power" (the power to produce results in you), "unto all patience and long-suffering with joyfulness." The believer will be strengthened to live in God's will with all patience; that is, keeping it up day by day, never quitting. "And long-suffering," which means enduring all "with joyfulness."

That last phrase is what usually gives trouble: to be able to be patient in the Lord and to be long-suffering in the Lord, with joy. The only way in the world we can have joy is to remember the Lord Jesus Christ. As we remember Him and have fellowship with Him, we will have joy.

REDEEMED
(Colossians 1:12–14)

Do you think just anybody as he is can share in all the blessing that comes through the gospel to a believer in Christ?

> Giving thanks unto the Father, which hath made us meet to be partakers of the inheritance of the saints in light: who hath delivered us from the power of darkness, and hath translated us into the kingdom of his dear Son: in whom we have redemption through his blood, even the forgiveness of sins (Col. 1:12–14).

Paul reminded the Colossian believers of his unceasing prayer for them. He wanted them to be fully appreciative of what God had done for them and would continue to do for them as believers. He wanted them to be filled with the knowledge of God's will in Christ, so that they could walk worthily in a strong, steadfast fashion. Paul pointed out that he gave thanks unto the Father, appreciating what He had done in His grace by sending Jesus Christ. Paul gave the Lord Jesus Christ supreme honors, but he knew that He would not have come into this world if the Father had not worked along with Him. Even today there is no way to preach the gospel soundly unless God is working with the preacher by His will and by His pleasure.

In Colossians 1:12–14 Paul gave thanks unto the Father, appreciating what God in grace had done. This word "meet" is an old English word of which we have almost lost the meaning, yet it is a proper word meaning "equal to." Paul referred to the fact that God has made us equal to this privilege, fit to receive this benefit. We may count that the "inheritance of the saints in light" would be like the benefits of the gospel. This is important as we shall notice. "Who hath delivered us from the power of darkness." Here we again have something important because this is a truth that we could easily miss. How was this done? Do you think this was just a matter of bookkeeping in that He just struck out the case against us, or is it actually like the other works of God—something that actually was performed? When and where did He deliver us from the power of darkness? This brings us directly to Calvary. He "hath delivered us from the power of darkness" on Calvary's cross where we were crucified with Him that we might be risen with Him. In one place we read, "crucified with Him" (Gal. 2:20), and in another place, "risen with Him" (Col. 2:12). This is what God is counting on, delivering us from the power of darkness by way of resurrection from the dead.

Death might very well be the work of darkness, and the power of darkness would be the power of death, from which we have been delivered by the resurrection. You will remember that Christ Jesus, bearing our sins in His own body, suffered unto death and died. He was crucified in weakness, as it were, unable to help Himself; and He died. But God raised Him from the dead, and when He raised Him from the dead it was to die no more. The penalty of sin had been paid and now He was delivered. "Hath delivered us from the power of darkness"—this took place at Calvary's cross. "Hath translated us into the kingdom of his dear Son"—this took place at the resurrection. The translation is "into Christ."

When we talk about living the resurrected life in Christ, let us keep in mind that being raised from the dead does not mean that we are being raised, then set down to go on doing as we have done. That was probably true about the resurrection of Lazarus and about the widow's son, but it is not true about the resurrection of the Lord Jesus Christ. When He was raised from the dead He was raised not to another life in this world but to a newness of life. What we have in the resurrection is not another human being now in gratitude surrendering himself to the Lord to seek to do His will, but we are being raised, regenerated, as members of the body of Christ. The idea that we are translated into the kingdom of His Son is very important, being translated by Calvary and the resurrection. The process of being redeemed and delivered from the power of darkness assures us we shall not die again.

Paul adds, "In whom we have redemption through his blood, even the forgiveness of sins." Redemption is a term that is taken from the money lenders; it has to do with a mortgage on a piece of property. The mortgage can be paid and the property redeemed. Our souls had something like a mortgage on them. We were obligated to die because of our sin. When Christ Jesus died for us, He paid the mortgage and removed the obligations occasioned by sin. Those obligations involved death. We have redemption through His blood shed at Calvary. He died, but God raised Him from the dead. If we believe in Him it is counted as though we had died. The obligations were removed and satisfied. Thus our sins are being expiated, and we are raised from the dead in Him.

CHRIST THE CREATOR
(Colossians 1:15–17)

How important is Jesus Christ compared with everyone else in the world?

> Who is the image of the invisible God, the first-born of every creature: for by him were all things created, that are in heaven, and that are in earth, visible and invisible, whether they be thrones, or dominions, or principalities, or powers: all things were created by him, and for him: and he is before all things, and by him all things consist (Col. 1:15–17).

There is no more remarkable statement in all literature about the importance of Jesus Christ: "Who is the image of the invisible God." We are told in John 14:8–9 that the Lord

Jesus was asked by one of the disciples, "Lord, show us the Father, and it sufficeth us. Jesus saith unto him, Have I been so long time with you, and yet hast thou not known me, Philip? He that hath seen me hath seen the Father." And you will remember in the book of Hebrews how, in chapter 1, verse 3 we read concerning Him that He is "the express image" of the invisible God. All of this brings to mind how that the Lord Jesus Christ in Himself actually was an exact and complete revelation of the Person of God. If you want to know what God looks like here in this world in humility, if you want to know what God looks like stripped of His power and His glory, then look at Jesus of Nazareth, for He is God.

Some time ago I heard a student preach on one of these verses. He made quite a point that in looking at the Person of the Lord Jesus Christ you could see the Creator of the world. From that he went on to say that when you looked into the face of the Babe at Bethlehem you saw the Creator of the world. I do not doubt that God is the Creator of the world. This very verse (Col. 1:16) tells us that the Lord Jesus Christ created all things, yet in the interest of avoiding confusion we would do well to remember that when the Lord Jesus became incarnate He laid aside His glory. He took a temporary position when He was made here in the form of man. But no matter how we may interpret that part of it, it still remains true that He is the image of the invisible God, the firstborn of every creature. The phrase "firstborn" means He is the most important One, superior to everything that is created.

Look at verse 16 more closely, "For by him were all things created." It can scarcely be made simpler. There we have the claim that all things were created by the Son of God who became incarnate as Jesus of Nazareth and was called the Christ. When Paul talks here about "all things," he makes it clear that he is referring to all things "that are in heaven." Several aspects are important with reference to the word "heaven." It is natural for us to have in mind some place a long distance away from this world, or an experience after we die and are raised from the dead. Still you must remember that while it is true that we will go to heaven, it has existed all the time. Heaven exists right now, even though you cannot point to the north, south, east, or west. It does not have a specific location, yet it is very real. It is so real the Lord Jesus could say,

> Let not your heart be troubled: ye believe in God, believe also
> in me. In my Father's house are many mansions: if it were not
> so, I would have told you. I go to prepare a place for you (John
> 14:1-2).

The word "heaven" does not refer only to some place to go after your body has been put in the grave. Heaven exists right now—"Our Father, which art in heaven."

The point Paul is making in this 16th verse is that all things in heaven were created by the Son of God. Look at the next phrase, "that are in earth." Then he discusses these things, "visible and invisible." Visible things would be the things of nature: mountains and trees, sun and moon, stars and all such things. Invisible things would have to do with that which cannot be seen: this would include the hearts of men, their loyalties and faithfulness, or their rebellions. God has made through Jesus Christ everything that is, "whether they be thrones, or dominions, or principalities, or powers." Everything that is was made by and through the power of Jesus the Son of God. "All things were created by him, and for him."

In verse 17 we read, "And he is before all things." He has a status above everything. He is above the crowd. He is first: at the very top. Paul also wrote, "and by him all things consist." That is a very important and interesting statement. You could have understood it more easily if Paul had said, "by him all things exist." That would mean that Christ Jesus gave them the power and the strength to be. But Paul wrote "all things consist" by Him. The word "consist" means the essence of their being is held together by the power of God. The One who is responsible for creating all things and holding them by the word of His power is none other than the Son of God, the Lord Jesus Christ. "Who is the image of the invisible God." Nothing can surpass that.

"For by him were all things created." Paul states that everything in heaven was made by this One, the Son of God. Also all things "that are in earth, visible and invisible, whether they be thrones, or dominions, or principalities, or powers: all things were created by him, and for him." Paul claimed that in Jesus Christ everything that "is" takes shape and form, and is held up by His power and strength. "And by him all things consist": all things hold together. This is how important Jesus Christ is in all creation.

Why bring all that in here? Christ Jesus is the Savior. He is the One in whom believers put their trust. He is the One who died for them. He is the One on whom they depend. He is the One believers are going to meet in heaven. He is praying for them. They can commit themselves to Him in all confidence.

CHRIST OVER ALL
(Colossians 1:18–20)

Do you realize what place in the universe is given to Jesus Christ by God Himself?

> And he is the head of the body, the church: who is the beginning, the firstborn from the dead; that in all things he might have the preeminence. For it pleased the Father that in him should all fulness dwell; and, having made peace through the blood of his cross, by him to reconcile all things unto himself; by him, I say, whether they be things in earth, or things in heaven (Col. 1:18–20).

In our last study we noted that during the time the Lord Jesus Christ was here upon earth in the incarnation, during the time He was Jesus of Nazareth, He was in His humiliation. His glory had been taken away, and He appeared in the form of a man. He took upon Himself the form of a servant to do a particular work. But all that time He really was the Son of God. We can remember that on the Mount of Transfiguration when Peter, James, and John were with Him they saw Him transformed before them. They saw His face shining like the noonday sun, and His clothing was glistening white. When they saw the Lord Jesus there, they were not seeing Him in any changed form—out of character for a few minutes. They actually saw the true Lord Jesus as He really was all the time.

This again comes to mind when we see here in the book of Colossians what the apostle Paul writes about the living Lord Jesus Christ. This high position of the Lord Jesus Christ was further noted in the remarks made by Paul in Colossians 1:18–20. Attention here is focused upon the work of Christ in the church. In verses 15 to 17 we saw how the emphasis was upon creation, and how Christ Jesus was the head of all things that were created. But here we see Him in relation to the church; the head of the body, the church. When the term "body" is used here it is not referring to an organized group, like a body of people living in a certain community or a body of people meeting in a certain hall or sanctuary. We are thinking of the way the Christian is related to the Lord Jesus Christ—as a member of the physical body is related to the head. This is used to accent our intimate relationship to the Lord Jesus Christ. He is the head and we are the members. He directs everything we do.

"Who is the beginning, the first-born from the dead" refers here to the church as the beginning of the new creation, the first-born from the dead. Whenever we think in the New Testament about the things of the gospel, we are to have in mind that God is doing something in Christ Jesus that had never been done before. When God works through the Lord Jesus Christ, He does not bring human beings to some high level of performance as human beings. He does not guide them as a community to achieving a high level of community performance. He calls men as individuals to put their trust in Him. In dying to self, being raised from the dead, living in newness of life, yielding to God, receiving the Holy Spirit, having the life of the Lord Jesus Christ in them, they become members of the church and are the beginning of the new creation. They are the first-born from the dead. Every single one is in resurrection life and in resurrection power: "That in all things he might have the pre-eminence."

Here Paul is laying emphasis upon the fact that as in verse 16 Christ has pre-eminence among all created things, so in verse 18 He has pre-eminence in the things that are in the new creation. The emphasis here is upon the relationship between Christ and all those who are raised. We can have in mind that men will continue their struggle to achieve rank and status over each other. They will be in conflict as one man will try to get ahead of another, but all the time there is one name above every name. This name no one can ever surpass because God has given Christ a name which is above every name, that "at the name of Jesus every knee should bow."

"For it pleased the Father that in him should all fullness dwell." Fullness of obedience is complete obedience to the will of God, which is in Jesus Christ. Fullness of love is a complete demonstration of the whole love of God in one Person, Jesus Christ. Fullness of faithfulness is being faithful in every little thing so as not to miss anything. The perfect record of obedience and faithfulness to God is in Jesus Christ: fullness in virtue because He never did anything wrong was found in Jesus Christ; fullness of wisdom in that Christ would know all things and could do anything because He is wise above all; fullness in strength because it pleased God the Father that in Jesus Christ all fullness should dwell.

"And, having made peace through the blood of his cross, by him to reconcile all things unto himself." This world, with all of its conflicts, is to be set aside through death. Through death we are to be delivered from this present evil world. Through the resurrection we are to enter into a new world wherein dwelleth righteousness, and where there is peace. Christ has made peace through the blood of His cross.

Nowhere in the Bible do we ever find that God brings peace to unbelieving men. There is no such thing as peace on earth among unregenerate people. When we speak of regenerated people, we are not speaking of human beings made perfect in themselves. Rather, they have died to self and have been raised by the power of God to live in the Son of God. Christ in them is the hope of glory. Such people will have peace. Thus there will be this wonderful peace of God which passeth all understanding.

RECONCILED TO GOD
(Colossians 1:21–23)

How can a man who is a sinner be brought to God?

> And you, that were sometime alienated and enemies in your mind by wicked works, yet now hath he reconciled in the body of his flesh through death, to present you holy and unblamable and unreprovable in his sight: if ye continue in the faith grounded and settled, and be not moved away from the hope of the gospel, which ye have heard, and which was preached to

every creature which is under heaven; whereof I Paul am made
a minister (Col. 1:21–23).

Sometimes we find church members who have lived
worldy lives before they became believers. It is very common also in our churches to have members who were born
into believing homes and brought up early to put their trust
in the Lord Jesus Christ. Many of these need to have a personal experience with the Lord Jesus Christ even though it
does not involve a dramatic conversion from a life of flagrant
sin. This is brought to mind when we read, "You, that were
sometime alienated and enemies in your mind by wicked
works, yet now hath he reconciled in the body of his flesh
through death." Each of us will have in mind that in Christ
Jesus we have been reconciled to God. As we read the book
of Colossians we remember all that has been done for us in
the name of Jesus Christ, and all that will be done for us in
His name.

When Paul speaks about being reconciled, this, of course,
means being reconciled to God and being brought into His
fellowship. We were like strangers and He brought us together "in the body of his flesh through death." There is
nothing to indicate here that my wayward, self-centered heart
was brought into fellowship with God or reconciled to Him.
As I was in my own human nature, I yielded myself to the
Lord Jesus Christ. I was to be crucified with Christ. What
part of me was crucified? That old rebellious, self-centered,
proud and conceited, contentious self. When I am raised from
the dead, I am raised in the Lord Jesus Christ. I am not raised
as a human being who will turn to the Lord Jesus Christ. I am
raised *in* the Lord Jesus Christ. When I come to consciousness as a born-again person I am a member of the body of the
Lord Jesus Christ. I now belong to God.

So we say about Christ that He has reconciled us in the
body of His flesh through death, "to present you holy and
unblamable and unreprovable in his sight." Now when He
presents me in this manner in His sight, this does not mean
that He is going to control me so that I will do everything I
should do. It means He will present me as I am, born again
with the life of Christ in me. I will be holy and unblamable
and unreprovable in His sight. The old man is dead on Cal-

vary's cross. The new man is Christ Jesus, who is acceptable to God the Father. This is emphasized in verse 23:

> If ye continue in the faith grounded and settled, and be not moved away from the hope of the gospel, which ye have heard, and which was preached to every creature which is under heaven; whereof I Paul am made a minister.

The marvelous prospect of being presented to God, holy, unblamable, unreprovable in His sight, being presented as His child, permanently and forever to be with Him is possible in the resurrection. As I yield myself to be crucified and risen with Christ, the new nature in me is what will be presented to God: holy, unblamable and unreprovable in His sight. Becoming a Christian is permanent when you enter into this relationship wherein you have Christ living in you forever. In "if you continue in the faith" the "if" is not so much a matter of doubt, raising the possibility that you won't be. You can translate that word "if" by using the word "since" or "inasmuch" as you continue in the faith, grounded and settled. What is grounded and settled is not the faith but you. If you, grounded and settled, continue in the faith, you will "be not moved away from the hope of the gospel."

What is that "hope of the gospel"? It is that you will have Christ Himself living in you. "When you are not moved away from" means that you will keep in mind all the time that you have the Lord Jesus Christ actually living in you. One might very well ask why that would be necessary. I think one reason is because the whole matter of being raised from the dead has not actually taken place in any overt fashion. We believe in the Lord Jesus Christ, but that means we always have opportunity to return to our former country if we want to (Heb. 11:15). This is emphasizing that the kind of faith that is saving faith is continuing faith. We need an enduring, persistent quality in our faith. In other words, when you accept Christ, you accept Him forever. When you turn to the Lord Jesus Christ, you do not turn to Him to merely escape from a problem, you turn to Him forever. Belonging to Him must be continuous if it is to be effectual.

CHRIST AT WORK IN US
(Colossians 1:24–27)

What is the principal truth in the gospel of Christ?

> Who now rejoice in my sufferings for you, and fill up that which
> is behind of the afflictions of Christ in my flesh for his body's
> sake, which is the church: whereof I am made a minister,
> according to the dispensation of God which is given to me for
> you, to fulfill the word of God; even the mystery which hath
> been hid from ages and from generations, but now is made
> manifest to his saints: to whom God would make known what is
> the riches of the glory of this mystery among the Gentiles;
> which is Christ in you, the hope of glory (Col. 1:24–27).

This is the basic principle and the underlying truth in the gospel of Christ; "Christ in you, the hope of glory." This truth, as Paul said, was hid from ages and from generations. It was not known before. As you read the Old Testament it would not occur to you that God's plan was eventually to accomplish the kind of performance in human beings He was looking for, by having them related to Him through Christ.

When we say this is the truth hidden from the ages and from generations in the past, it is somewhat like a rosebush growing in your yard. It looks like a little shrub with its woody branches. You could not tell then that it will have a beautiful rose on it. That beautiful rose is hidden from view during the spring of the year but it will eventually be seen. In Old Testament days the development of the truth that God's plan was to include that His Son, Christ the Messiah, would be in God's people performing God's will was hidden from view.

Now is the time for us to recognize that being a believer in Christ is not a matter of virtue. A person is not a believer in Christ because he is better than somebody else. It is not a matter of ethics; it is not a matter even of service. Being a believer in Christ is primarily a matter of having Christ, the living Lord Jesus Christ, active and operative in you. There are things to learn about what Christ would have us do. The important truth in being a believer in Christ is that Christ Jesus is active in us by the Holy Spirit.

Now let us look more closely at this passage. Paul suffered as a preacher of the gospel, but this suffering was incidental to the fact that he preached the Word which enabled the souls who heard him to believe and to call upon God. Since his preaching enabled those souls to believe and to call upon God, Paul accepted his sufferings gladly. "Who now rejoice in my sufferings for you." He interpreted those personal afflictions in his ministry as being caused by his preaching the gospel. He therefore considered that his own personal sufferings were a sort of reminder of Christ's sufferings. Paul rejoiced because he was sharing with others the truth about the Lord Jesus Christ, enabling them to believe and to be saved.

"Whereof I am made a minister." Apparently this refers to the church of which he was made a "minister," which means "a servant." He was made a minister of this truth in the church "according to the dispensation of God which is given to me for you, to fulfill the word of God." In other words, Paul was made a minister, a servant of the Lord Jesus Christ, to fulfill the Word of God. He was to facilitate what God wanted to have done. God's promises in Christ Jesus are for everyone who believes. This is the function of any minister, and he is to fulfill the Word of God, bringing it through to its completeness and fruitfulness in believers.

> Even the mystery which hath been hid from ages and from generations, but now is made manifest to his saints: to whom God would make known what is the riches of the glory of this mystery among the Gentiles; which is Christ in you, the hope of glory.

This is the great truth, the blossom on the rosebush. This is what really makes the difference. God wants us to know finally and fully that Christ will be in us, working in us; we can then expect the will of God to be done in us. "Christ in you, the hope of glory" is the ground on which we can expect to be glorified. This is the basis on which we can hope to do the will of God. "Christ in you" is the hope we have that we will enter into the glory of God. Let us never miss this truth. We need to always remember that the basic thing in being a believer in Christ is to have the Lord Jesus Christ working in our hearts.

PREACHING WITH A PURPOSE
(Colossians 1:28–29)

Do you have any idea what a minister of Christ really wants to accomplish in his hearers?

> Whom we preach, warning every man, and teaching every man in all wisdom; that we may present every man perfect in Christ Jesus: whereunto I also labor, striving according to his working, which worketh in me mightily (Col. 1:28–29).

The apostle Paul left no doubt in the minds of anybody that what he was undertaking was to set before human beings the truth of the Christ of the Bible. God's great plan for saving men is through His chosen Servant, His Messiah. The minister of the gospel discusses an absent Lord. But he talks about Him as an indwelling Christ because, although Christ in His body is at the right hand of God, it is possible for fellowship to occur between the individual believer and the living Lord Jesus Christ. Paul says, "Whom we preach." This is what he kept telling people always, that Christ Jesus was available for anybody who would turn to Him; that He would save whoever came to God by Him.

We might ask ourselves why he would warn believers. It would be easy for me to make the mistake of imagining that what God wanted was that I should do right in His sight. That is a simple and easy snare to fall into. It is true as far as it goes, but it is not the gospel truth. It is true that God wants me to do right, but the truth is that I do not do right. The truth is that I *was* a sinner. I *am* a sinner. I *will be* a sinner. Because that is the case, I am condemned. "There is none righteous, no not one." I am no different from other people. I do not have it in me to be right or to do right. (See Romans 3:10, 23).

But let us hear the gospel. God sent His Son Jesus Christ to be the Savior of sinners. Christ Jesus does in Himself, in His death and resurrection, what is necessary to make possible that "whosoever believeth in Him shall not perish but have everlasting life" (John 3:16). If I believe these things and commit myself to them, the Bible says God will regenerate me, make me a new creature in Christ Jesus, adopt me into His family as one of His children, and put His Holy Spirit in my heart so Christ will become active in me. All of this will be

done for me. Thus I become a believer in Christ. Then I will
do the right thing, not because I am doing it, but because
Christ is in me the hope of glory. He does it.

When Paul preached, he preached Christ. He warned
everyone not to make the natural mistake, which could be
avoided if a person was conscious of it. The natural mistake is
thinking that he can do it and that he is to do it. Paul writes,
"teaching every man in all wisdom." This truth needs to be
known to guide the believer's growth in Christ Jesus.

What then is our peril? We are in danger that we will
undertake to do the will of God in our own strength. This we
cannot do. It is the born-again, regenerated man who is
adopted as a child of God and is given the Holy Spirit, even as
the air is given to a newborn infant. Every believer in Christ
is such a person who can do the will of God. The believer in
Christ has two natures: one nature is called the flesh, the
other nature is called the spirit. In the believer all the things
of the flesh are interested in the things of self, and the things
of the spirit are interested in the things of Christ. A believer
in Christ can be torn between the two.

Paul warns not to try in the flesh to do the will of God. To
perform the will of God in my own strength is impossible.
"There is no man that sinneth not." A man must avoid being
taken in by the flesh, and Paul warns against such hopeless
efforts.

Paul labored to present every man perfect in Christ Jesus.
The word "perfect" means mature; understanding everything.
Paul labored to bring his flock into such a relationship with
Christ that they would understand that in the presence of God
they were counted righteous. And Christ Himself worked in
the believers to bring this to pass. So Paul preached Christ,
warning and teaching in all wisdom "that we may present
every man perfect in Christ Jesus." Paul wanted to present
every man mature, completely understanding his relationship
in Christ Jesus. "Whereunto I also labor, striving according to
his working, which worketh in me mightily."

Here the apostle is saying that even his preaching is not his
own, nor his praying, nor even his concern. God is working in
him to will and to do of His good pleasure. The very preaching
Paul did was part of God's way of saving souls.

CHAPTER 2

† † †

UNDERSTANDING GOD
(Colossians 2:1-3)

Do you understand what Paul really wanted for his Christian followers?

> For I would that ye knew what great conflict I have for you, and for them at Laodicea, and for as many as have not seen my face in the flesh; that their hearts might be comforted, being knit together in love, and unto all riches of the full assurance of understanding, to the acknowledgment of the mystery of God, and of the Father, and of Christ; in whom are hid all the treasures of wisdom and knowledge (Col. 2:1-3).

The apostle Paul writes as though to say to the Colossians: "I only wish you knew what I am trying to bring to pass in your hearts." In our studies so far we have been noting truth about the believer's experience. Paul has been striving to help the believers in Christ, who are like his church members, to achieve spiritual experience. We learn from what the apostle has written thus far that the essence of being a believer in Christ is one's relationship with the living Lord. It is a matter of receiving Christ Jesus in the heart. This is difficult because we are dealing with things that are invisible. It is easy for a human being to misunderstand the meaning of the words he hears.

One can understand how this might happen. Naturally a man wants his own will to be done, but God wants His way to be followed. What God wants in the whole program of salvation is that His will eventually be done. "He that doeth the will of God shall abide forever" (1 John 2:17). A believer's mistake may be that he will try in his own strength to do God's will. This is a waste of time and a frustration for the spirit.

Paul preached the truth about man, then he agonized to bring it to pass in the hearts of his hearers: it is "Christ in you" that is the hope of glory. Paul was much in prayer about this for these believing souls; that they might be comforted in this great truth, "being knit together in love."

First of all, there is the love of God for us in that God loves all people. But He particularly loves those who put their trust in Him. So all believers who trust in the Lord Jesus Christ share in the love of the Father. They are drawn together, and their hearts are comforted, "being knit together in love, and unto all riches of the full assurance of understanding, to the acknowledgment of the mystery of God, and of the Father, and of Christ."

What Paul wanted was for these people to really understand the meaning of their relationship with God in Christ Jesus. This was the essence of their strength as believers in Christ. What really matters in the heart of the believer is that he understands about God and His ways, about Christ and about the gospel, "to the acknowledgment of the mystery of God, and of the Father, and of Christ."

As brought out before, the word "mystery" means hidden truth. There is something true about God for the believer in Christ that the casual reader of the Bible will not see; but it is there and every believer in Christ can recognize it. It is to be found in the two words "Father" and "Christ." "Of the Father, and of Christ." Christ is the Old Testament term used for the Savior of Israel: the One who would come to save God's people. When the word "Father" is used with reference to God, we should think in terms of the Son, because nobody can be a father who does not have a child.

The real hidden truth about God is that the Christ, the Anointed One in Old Testament times who would save the people of Israel, would be the Son of God. God would be His Father because He would be begotten of God. This is the actual truth that would save Israel, and this is the great truth for believers in Christ today. God so loved the world that He sent His only begotten Son, who was Jesus of Nazareth. The outstanding truth about Jesus of Nazareth that makes Him the Son of God is that He was not born of human parents. He was born of God: conceived by the Holy Spirit in the virgin Mary.

He is our Savior. He is the Savior of the world. This is a
pattern for believers because it is exactly how they will come
to God. This is the gospel. When any one of us comes to God,
we come by believing in the Lord Jesus Christ, and by being
born again. What do we mean by the term "born again"?
"Begotten again of the Word and of the Spirit" and "Begotten
of God."

So God is our Father because we have been begotten of
Him. He is not our Father because of what He does for us. He
is not our Father because He created us. He is not our Father
because He gives to us. God is our Father because we are
born of Him, and we live in Him. God will become our Father
as we are born again of Him by His Holy Spirit. To know this
is to be comforted and to be assured and to be strong.

COLOSSIANS IN CHRIST
(Colossians 2:4–5)

Do you realize that the main element in a believer's experience is his faith in Christ?

> And this I say, lest any man should beguile you with enticing
> words. For though I be absent in the flesh, yet am I with you in
> the spirit, joying and beholding your order, and the steadfast-
> ness of your faith in Christ (Col. 2:4–5).

In these words the apostle indicates that what really con-
cerns him is that young believers could be led to wrong ideas
and to wrong activities. He was alarmed lest these young
believers in Colossae be misled by people who would preach
and teach what was not true. There are false guides who can
and do use enticing words. The truth of the gospel is simple,
and nobody needs to wonder what it means. But the truth of
the gospel is humbling. It demands faith because the revelation of the gospel as it is brought to us is that salvation is by
the power of God, not by our efforts. Salvation is something
that is done for us, in us, and through us, by Christ Himself.

It is pleasing to the human ego to be made to feel that we
can do the will of God. There are those who teach in such a
way as to imply that we can do it. They flatter us into thinking

that we can do it. Then we feel we should do it. We then spend our time and work hard and get nowhere before we realize that we could not do it in the first place. The Colossians had not yet embraced such a mistaken view. Paul rejoiced as he took note of their order and the steadfastness of their faith in love. Notice verse 5, "For though I be absent in the flesh, yet am I with you in the spirit." He meant to say, "I am able to sense the whole situation. I can feel it"—"joying and beholding your order." He rejoiced and noted their discipline, their self-control. They were humbly waiting for Christ to lead them, not expecting to do it in themselves.

Paul is reminding them that salvation has come because Christ works in them by His power. This is the significance of being a child of God. "And the steadfastness of your faith in Christ." Notice that word "Christ." Here I want to make you thoughtful of something: we should be very careful that we do not use the word "Jesus" in this connection. Actually it is not faith in Jesus of Nazareth while He was living in this world that is going to save the soul. It is faith in "Christ" who died, was raised from the dead and taken into heaven. Remember how Peter said on the Day of Pentecost, "God hath made that same Jesus both Lord and Christ" (Acts 2:36). For a long time this had been known in the early church, before Paul wrote to the Colossians. But this was that in which the Colossians put their trust.

This is the route you take when you are being saved. You deny yourself, take your flesh to the cross, and when you are then buried you forsake yourself. After this you are raised from the dead, not to be the same kind of person you were before, but to be a member of the body of Christ. So you rejoice in that. This is what it means to have your faith in Christ. The Lord Jesus was not only raised from the dead but was taken into the very presence of God. There He sits at the right hand of God, and there in Spirit we are reconciled to God, actually being in His very presence.

All of this is included in the faith in Christ. These people were steadfast about it. They talked about yielding themselves to the indwelling Christ, who would serve His Father. This is the way of salvation, and the Colossian Christians were convinced this was true.

THE WAY TO WALK
(Colossians 2:6-7)

Do you understand there are certain things one should know in order to live the life of faith in Christ?

> As ye have therefore received Christ Jesus the Lord, so walk ye in him: rooted and built up in him, and stablished in the faith, as ye have been taught, abounding therein with thanksgiving (Col. 2:6-7).

This is a simple exhortation. It is as though a person were to say something like this, "Now that you are married, make it a point to set up your home," or "Now that you have joined the army, start acting like a soldier." You were not always a believer in Christ, and you were not always depending upon Him, but you did receive Christ Jesus as Lord, so walk ye in Him with the same understanding you had when you received Him. Let us again remind ourselves that as we are born once into this world as human beings, so we must be born again of the water and the spirit that we may be children of God in Christ Jesus. "But as many as received him, to them gave he power to become the sons of God, even to them that believe on his name" (John 1:12).

Here we see emphasis upon receiving Christ, "As ye have therefore received Christ Jesus the Lord, so walk ye in him." This is a way of asking what you were thinking about when you accepted Jesus Christ. Well, now live it out that way. We will see that living as a believer in Christ demands that we have information. A person who has never heard the gospel cannot do it. You need to practice diligence about the information that you have. It is true that anybody can be a believer in Christ. "Whosoever will may come," but not in just any way. It will have to be in God's way. There is no such thing as living the spiritual life alone; you need to have the Lord. So the apostle asked what they were thinking about when they received Him, and admonished them to keep on thinking about that as they walked with Him and lived with Him.

"As ye have therefore received Christ Jesus the Lord." Let us look again briefly at those three names. The word "Jesus" refers to His earthly career. "Thou shalt call his name Jesus, for he shall save his people from their sins" (Matt. 1:21). Jesus is the One who lived in Galilee; the One they arrested and hanged on the tree. So there is a very real sense in which, when you say the word "Jesus," you are talking about your Savior and your Sacrifice. "Christ" has more to do with the function He performs in bringing us to God. He is our Mediator, and when the Lord Jesus was raised from the dead and came into the presence of God, Peter could say, "God hath made that same Jesus, whom ye have crucified, both Lord and Christ" (Acts 2:36). Christ is the Old Testament name for the Messiah, the One who would come to deliver His people. And so the word "Christ" refers to our Mediator, our Advocate. The word "Lord" speaks of Someone who will direct you, who will be the captain of your soul. So when you receive Christ Jesus the Lord, you receive Christ as your Mediator, Jesus as your Sacrifice, and the Lord as your Leader.

When a person sins he must bring a sacrifice and confess his sins. The same Lord Jesus Christ is even now interceding on your behalf, confessing your sins. Because Christ is your Mediator, you can confide in Him, you can trust Him and follow Him. Because He is your Leader, you can concur and obey His will. "As ye have therefore received Christ Jesus the Lord," now live that way.

Notice the rest of verse 7, "Rooted and built up in him, and stablished in the faith." The word "rooted" suggests the forgiveness of sins. You have received the forgiveness of sins and are rooted in Him. You will be edified as you are obedient to His will. When you think of being built up in Him, you have been developed and strengthened in Him as you have obeyed His will.

"And stablished in the faith, as ye have been taught." You accepted the orientation of the faith as it was presented; now you are rooted, built up in Him, stablished in the faith. These things were given to you. You would not have found them out by yourself. Some witness brought them to you.

"Abounding therein with thanksgiving." The word "abounding" indicates eagerness. You eagerly follow the guidance you have from the Lord, turning to Him at all times, seeking His favor, and gladly yielding to the Word of God. When you practice thanksgiving for the things which have happened in the past, you are preparing yourself for the future.

In this portion of Colossians there are set forth instructions as to how believers in Christ are to live. They are to give themselves over completely to walking with the Lord.

DON'T BE DECEIVED!
(Colossians 2:8–9)

Is there danger to a person's spiritual life because of thoughts expressed by unbelievers?

> Beware lest any man spoil you through philosophy and vain deceit, after the tradition of men, after the rudiments of the world, and not after Christ. For in him dwelleth all the fullness of the Godhead bodily (Col. 2:8–9).

When we read the word "beware" there is a warning that means take note and be very careful. "Lest any man spoil you." This word "spoil" could well be written "despoil," a word taken from military experience. This would be a person who would take away from you what you have, like the spoils of war.

If you are a believer in Christ and you have faith in the Lord so that you are counting on Him, this means that as a believer in Christ you know that Christ Jesus died for your sins, that you are forgiven, and that right now the Lord Jesus is alive and interceding for you in the presence of God. All these things are in your mind. They are not the ordinary thoughts of the public. Paul warned that the believer must be careful lest anybody despoil or rob him through philosophy and vain deceit. This does not say necessarily that philosophy is wrong; whether it is right or wrong is quite another matter altogether. Whether it is useful or useless is a particular problem. But it is in the general area of philosophizing that there are people who will despoil you, taking away the ideas which you have embraced.

"Vain deceit" is when people are empty in their pride; "after the tradition of men" because everybody else is doing it; "after the rudiments of the world," because it fits in with this particular world "and not after Christ." The believer in Christ is to be very careful about this. Ordinarily speaking a person may say that he does not care anything about philosophy. But do you listen to explanations or arguments? By the way, where you see this word "philosophy" you can put the word "psychology," "social science" and "psychiatry." A believer in Christ must be very careful lest somebody rob him through a sophisticated, intellectual way of looking at things. "Vain deceit" means a person's pretending to know things because he wants to have his name big, when he actually does not know what he is talking about. A person could present a strong argument that would show you, according to certain books, that what you believe is not true; you may listen to the argument until you doubt what you have. Then you would not have it any more; you would have lost it. The philosopher seldom makes any effort to really prove his point. He tries to show you that what you think cannot possibly be true, and there are others who possibly have better ideas. It is a fact that in this area of intellectual consideration people can begin to lose what they have cherished. This is particularly true in colleges where a student gets philosophy from all angles, with the consequence that he no longer has any faith. When he loses his faith he ignores and neglects the things of the Lord Jesus Christ.

"After the rudiments of the world." In 1 John 2:16 we read about "the lust of the flesh, and the lust of the eyes, and the pride of life." These are the rudiments of the world. The person who, in his thinking, is influenced by what he would like to see, what he would like to feel, and what he would like to be, so that all these things that have to do with the flesh and with pride and vanity are in his mind, no longer thinks of the things of the Spirit. He is now following after the rudiments of the world and not after Christ.

If a person is following Christ, he will deny himself. Christ Jesus lived in this world and did not do as He pleased. He did what His Father wanted Him to do. If a person walks along with Christ, that is what he will do. If he does not come humbly before the Lord and yield to Him but starts figuring on being smart enough to understand and be able to explain "philosophy and vain deceit," he can be robbed.

All the ways of the world are an abomination in the sight of the Lord. If a person follows Christ, he is humble before God.

He has yielded himself to God. He has put his trust in God. But when a person is full of self and pride and arrogance and intellectual sophistication, he is not humble before God. "For in him dwelleth all the fullness of the Godhead bodily." The believer in Christ stays with the things of the Lord Jesus Christ. He walks with Him in all the fullness of God. So far as love, grace and humility are concerned, the believer will have all the fullness of God. So far as compassion and integrity are concerned, he will have all the fullness of God. This is what the believer has in Christ Jesus.

ALL TO HIM I OWE
(Colossians 2:10–12)

Do you realize that everything a believer in Christ has that will affect him for good is something he receives from the Lord Jesus Christ?

> And ye are complete in him, which is the head of all principality and power: in whom also ye are circumcised with the circumcision made without hands, in putting off the body of the sins of the flesh by the circumcision of Christ: buried with him in baptism, wherein also ye are risen with him through the faith of the operation of God, who hath raised him from the dead (Col. 2:10–12).

In our previous study Paul warned about the danger that someone might rob the Colossian Christians of their blessing in Christ. Here he makes a straightforward affirmation, "And ye are complete in him, which is the head of all principality and power." The average humble person can feel inferior when a sophisticated, educated individual starts discussing his simple faith. The apostle Paul here puts a floor under the believer, something he can stand on. He does not attempt to meet that danger with a long argument, but with a simple direct affirmation. He is saying, "You have the Lord, and when you have Him you have everything. You may not be very strong, but He is. You may not be very important, but He is. You may not be very faithful, but He is faithful."

Notice the phrase "ye are circumcised with the circumcision made without hands." Unless one is trained in the Scriptures he scarcely would know how to interpret this. Circumcision was a ceremony that was introduced in the time of Abraham when he received the promise from God. In the Old Testament, circumcision was very much as it is with us when we baptize infants. Circumcision was something the parents did with the children when they committed them to God. The apostle uses this as a figure of speech when he writes that believers have been marked, as it were committed to Christ, with the circumcision that was made without hands. It was not a physical but an inward circumcision that happened to the believer when he put off the sins of the flesh by the circumcision of Christ. When the believer received Christ into his soul he was stamped before God. He belonged to God as truly as a Jew belonged to the family of Abraham when he had been circumcised.

Paul is referring not to some outward ceremony conducted by man but to a real spiritual experience in which, as the believer receives Christ Jesus, he is counted as having been committed to Christ. Christ had been circumcised. He personally yielded Himself to, and belonged to God. When the believer receives Christ, that is brought over, as it were, into the believer's life. In a general way the believer is to have the thought that he is circumcised with the circumcision of Christ. Everything the Lord Jesus did in the fulfilling of the law was done, as it were, on behalf of the believer.

"Buried with him in baptism." When the believer was baptized into the Lord Jesus Christ, then Christ's burial became his burial. There is a real sense in which at the time of the believer's burial, in Christ's burial, he forsakes everything of this world. We can have in mind with reference to the grave that the person who is buried "can't take it with him." He must leave everything of this world behind him. Just as you will leave everything of this world behind when you die, so when you give yourself to Jesus Christ you leave all the things that are away from God behind you. "Ye are risen with him through the faith of the operation of God, who hath raised him from the dead." When the soul believes in the Lord Jesus Christ, it is counted in the sight of God as though that soul had been raised with Christ. God begins to deal with the believer that way.

So Paul saw the believers as circumcised and committed to God (they belonged to God just the way Isaac belonged to Abraham, and the way the Lord Jesus belonged to the Father). They belonged now to God because they had been circumcised with the circumcision of Christ. When the believers received Christ, they inherited what He had. Since this was already done, the believers were complete in Him. Paul emphasized here that they belonged to God. Nothing could hurt them; nobody could touch them. They were complete in Him.

COMPLETE IN CHRIST
(Colossians 2:13–15)

Do you realize that spiritual life is based on what has been done for the believer and to him, and not on what he is going to do?

> And you, being dead in your sins and the uncircumcision of your flesh, hath he quickened together with him, having forgiven you all trespasses; blotting out the handwriting of ordinances that was against us, which was contrary to us, and took it out of the way, nailing it to his cross; and having spoiled principalities and powers, he made a show of them openly, triumphing over them in it (Col. 2:13–15).

Far too often our whole outlook on spiritual living is in terms of what we plan to do. We may seek to win other people to accept Christ as if we were going to enlist them in a project of some sort. This is not New Testament procedure at all. Certain people are believers in Christ because something has been done for them that is so real, so sure, and so final they can rest quietly and be at peace. They belong to God. Being a believer in Christ has to be something like this: if you should happen to be a sick person, and on your deathbed you would turn to God in Christ Jesus, humbly and penitently, committing yourself to Christ, and trusting Him, you are to understand that "this day shalt thou be with me in paradise" (Luke 23:43). Suppose you are afflicted, having suffered a stroke which completely paralyzed you. Do you realize you could become a believer in Christ even though you could not move out of your bed? Being a believer in Christ is not based on what you do; being a believer in Christ is based on something God has already done for you. The apostle stresses this because he wants the Colossian believers to be sure about it.

Confidence and assurance are based upon the finished work of Christ. Because that is so, the believer is free: yet he completely belongs to Christ. The resurrection of the Lord Jesus Christ is an established event, not something that is going to happen or that might happen. And that is the sure basis for our whole outlook as believers in Christ.

In verse 13 the language is strange but the ideas can be understood. All Paul has written has to do with the resurrection from the dead. The phrase, "being dead in your sins and the uncircumcision of your flesh, hath he quickened together with him, having forgiven you all trespasses," has to do with the resurrection from the dead. The word "dead" is a very important word. It does not mean that the person is obliterated or wiped out. The body can be lying in the casket but the auditory nerve does not carry a message; light can shine in the room but the optic nerve does not respond.

You, being dead, were at one time like that in sins and the uncircumcision of your flesh. As a human being you had no interest in the things of God. You could not have understood them if you had wanted to. "Hath he quickened together with him." The word "quickened" is an old English word that means "made alive," and that is what happened at the resurrection. Christ Jesus came alive. One way we use that expression in the ordinary conversation is when we refer to trees in the northern part of the country, in the spring of the year. We say they "quicken" when the buds burst open. Christ has revived us, having resurrected us from the dead with Himself. We now have a certain hope for the future.

The two expressions, "being dead in your sins and the uncircumcision of your flesh" refer to a certain condition of deadness: unresponsiveness now and a certain hopelessness for the future. "Quickened" has a certain significance of sensitiveness and a hopefulness for the future, knowing that you will also be raised. "Having forgiven you all trespasses." No matter how dull a person may be, when he is forgiven, everything his heart desires will begin to stir.

"Blotting out the handwriting of ordinances that was against us, which was contrary to us, and took it out of the way, nailing it to his cross." The "us" refers to us as sinners, "blotting out the handwriting of ordinances that was against us [back in the days when we were dead in trespasses and sin], which was contrary to us" [as we were as human beings], "and took it out of the way, nailing it to his cross; and having spoiled principalities and powers" [having robbed them without pay. The Lord Jesus Christ spoiled principalities and powers in the sense of death spoiling them, robbing them of their prey. When He delivered you and me and robbed Satan of his prey] "he made a show of them openly." [He put on the display by being raised from the dead] "triumphing over them in it." In what? "The handwriting of the ordinances that were against us."

In other words, as sinners we were in real trouble; we had everything against us; we were under condemnation and bondage and could expect nothing but the punishment that would come upon us. But Christ made a show of the forces against us, triumphing over them by setting us free. And Christ set us free by means of the resurrection. A person dies because of sin; he is raised from the dead by the power of God. In that way God robbed Satan of his prey. All of this simply means that believers in Christ are absolutely free because Christ was raised from the dead.

WHAT REALLY COUNTS
(Colossians 2:16–17)

Do you understand in what sense it is true that a believer in Christ does not live by regulations?

> Let no man therefore judge you in meat, or in drink, or in respect of a holy-day, or of the new moon, or of the sabbath days: which are a shadow of things to come, but the body is of Christ (Col. 2:16–17).

If a person knows what is in the Bible he will know what he can expect from God. It will give him reason for trusting, and for guidance because he believes in God. Generally speaking, believing people are inclined to be humble folks. The person who believes in the Lord Jesus Christ for his salvation is a person who has given up on himself; he thinks of himself as a sinner. Before Almighty God he can say, "Lord be merciful to me, a sinner," and this causes him humbly to have the feeling that he could easily be wrong about things. Because of this, it is natural for a believer to be sensitive to the criticism and to the pressure of other people.

There are believers whose spiritual experience is handicapped because other people interfere with them. Such persons put the believers under certain restrictions which are really not from the Lord but only from people. This is brought out clearly in this particular passage. The apostle is saying to the Colossian believers that in view of what he has just been telling them in the second chapter they are complete in the Lord Jesus Christ. Everything has been done and they truly are saved.

Paul now says, "Let no man therefore judge you" (that is, criticize you) "in meat" (that is, with reference to your food). The religious customs of the day were such as would cause one to feel it was right to eat certain food but not right to eat other food. Food was considered ceremonially clean or unclean. There was food that we call "kosher," and other food that was "not kosher." Believers could be criticized if they ate food of any kind that was not cleansed. The apostle states they should not let anybody criticize them because of the food they ate, on the basis of religious rules and regulations. This principle will carry over to common practices in our day.

Now Paul goes on to add, "or in drink." There were people in those days who said it was not right to drink wine or certain other kinds of liquor. Paul is saying here nobody should criticize them for what they drank because of religious reasons or in respect of a holy day. Even today there are people who feel that Christmas should be specially recognized. They want to act on Christmas day as if it were Sunday. But there is no such day as Christmas in the Bible, and there is no such day given in the gospel itself. Paul is telling the believers not to feel responsible to anybody about keeping such religious customs.

Paul continues, "or of the new moon." This practice is

largely unknown to us. In those days there were certain things people felt should be done every new moon, and certain things that should not be done every new moon. "Or of the sabbath days." There were certain ceremonial rules about what activity was allowed on the Sabbath Day—how much work one could do and how far one could walk. "Which are a shadow of things to come." Now the word "shadow" means, as you know, a reflection, a representation of things to come. Such clean and unclean designations as have been listed in verse 16 are indicative of religious or obedient living. They are signs of a truly yielded life. But the real thing is to have a personal relationship with Christ.

Wherever there is a group of sincere believers, a denomination or a congregation or even a family, it is normal that certain judgments about actions on their part will become standardized. There will be some things they will do and some things they will not do. There are people who think one should wear no jewelry; others do not believe in the radio or T.V. They think of these things as being sinful. They think of tobacco or any kind of spirituous liquor or dancing or playing cards as being sinful. Any one or all of these things are shadows of the real thing. They are reflections of real commitment but their practice can become artificial. It is personal communion with Christ that counts—the inward, heartfelt obedience to Him that really matters. Paul is anxious that these believers in Christ should realize that true obedience is more inward than outward observance; however, this does not mean that he would favor license. A mature believer will seek to please Christ.

Pleasing Christ may well mean that a believer will not gamble, or that he will not drink liquor. Pleasing Christ may well mean a believer will do none of these things. The apostle Paul said, "Wherefore, if meat make my brother to offend, I will eat no flesh while the world standeth, lest I make my brother to offend" (1 Cor. 8:13). A believer in Christ who is inwardly in fellowship with the Lord Jesus Christ may observe rules. He remembers that when the Lord Jesus Christ came to John the Baptist to be baptized and John said, "You don't need it," He replied, "It becometh us to fulfill all righteousness" (Matt. 3:15).

You and I do not want to live in a loose fashion; we want to recognize that some things are good and some bad, but our personal relationship with the Lord is what really counts.

DON'T BE FOOLED
(Colossians 2:18–19)

Do you realize that a person can act very religious and yet not be a believer in Christ?

> Let no man beguile you of your reward in a voluntary humility and worshiping of angels, intruding into those things which he hath not seen, vainly puffed up by his fleshly mind, and not holding the Head, from which all the body by joints and bands having nourishment ministered, and knit together, increaseth with the increase of God (Col. 2:18–19).

The apostle continued to discuss with these believers what it meant to have fellowship with the Lord Jesus Christ, and what it meant to live in obedience to Him. What Paul discussed at this time was the fact that there are people who act in a religious manner who are not really obedient to the Lord. Almost everyone is acquainted with people who know the Bible well, yet they are not desirable persons. There are people like that with reference to religion. Some have humble and gentle ways of doing things, but they act that way for purposes entirely their own and not particularly to please the Lord.

Paul is anxious that these young believers in Christ should not be taken in by folks who act religiously, but who do not have a personal relationship with the Lord Jesus Christ. Those who become believers in Christ will do certain things: they will go to church, read their Bible daily and they may have a certain time for the family altar. They serve the Lord and give to His work. But there can be persons who will do all these things for the purpose of acting as if they were religious. In these verses, Paul urged that believers in Christ strive to be genuine. What he said in this passage is that outward conduct is not so important. Some persons will show affection publicly, while some may feel that the personal demonstration of affection between husband and wife should be private.

There are people who are like that with religion. One man can go to church because it is good for his business: he makes it a point to talk to certain people because during the week he will have business dealings with them. The apostle Paul would be very stern in judging a man along those lines.

"Let no man beguile you of your reward." The word "beguile" means to lead you wrong. What is your reward? In the Sermon on the Mount, the Lord Jesus said that if you do things like giving to the poor to be seen of men, verily you will have your reward. Men will praise you but God will not. However, if you give to people secretly as unto the Lord, He will honor you for it. So it is with prayer. There are some who think that because praying may make them look as though they are religious, they pray openly. We remember how Jesus of Nazareth spoke of the hypocrites: they prayed in the synagogues and in the streets and made long prayers to be seen of men. The Lord Jesus said, "Verily, they have their reward." They are seen of men and they get whatever credit they receive in that way, but not from God.

Now the reward would be blessing from God. Paul urged, "Do not let anybody fool you into missing this blessing." A person can miss the blessing if he goes through the motions without meaning what he is doing. Paul continued, "in a voluntary humility." The word "voluntary" means free will, and you know what humility means. I am sure you are conscious of this, but among all the people you know, do you know anybody who puts on an act about being humble? Have you ever dealt with people like that? When you are with them they act humble and gentle and one could easily be led to think it is real. But others who live with those people can tell you that when at home they are not a bit like that.

"And worshiping of angels." Here I am going to comment that actually this worshiping of angels would be giving credit to those who bring the message—giving credit to spiritual forces that may affect you who are less than Christ. Such angels are messengers of the gospel. They can show a humility that is affected. Paul is warning against any act of giving credit to or even reverence to such messengers. These may speak of things that are spiritual in nature, but they do not really belong to the Lord.

"Intruding into those things which he hath not seen, vainly puffed up by his fleshly mind." There are persons who will deal with this whole matter of spiritual life and experience, and who will talk about a spiritual relationship with God, but they do not talk about the Lord Jesus Christ. They may explain how you can worship God and serve Him by certain things you could do: bowing your head in a certain way, repeating words and phrases and participating in rituals. All this can be done without thinking about the Lord Jesus Christ. The apostle Paul would say that hearers will miss the truth: they will be getting something that is human, and that is all. If teachers are "not holding the Head" (not respecting the Lord Jesus Christ or depending upon Him), they will miss the real truth. The fact is that the indwelling Lord Jesus Christ will keep you. And the "joints and bands" in the body would be individual members who serve to help others grow. The whole church will grow in grace and knowledge because each person is conscious of the Lord Jesus Christ and respects Him.

The apostle Paul warned, "Be very careful" about those who go around the country and are counted as religious, but who do not honor Jesus Christ. Remember this: if you are taken in by human acts in this way, you will miss the blessing of God.

RULED BY CHRIST
(Colossians 2:20–22)

Can you understand how it is that if a believer in Christ is truly obedient to Christ he will not need rules or regulations made by men?

> Wherefore if ye be dead with Christ from the rudiments of the world, why, as though living in the world, are ye subject to ordinances, (touch not; taste not; handle not; which all are to perish with the using;) after the commandments and doctrines of men (Col. 2:20–22)?

What is Paul saying? He is saying something like this: if a girl gets married why would she make dates with young men?

You say that is out of the question! Of course it is. If she has just married, why would she look at advertisements about a boarding house or why would she be interested in finding a girl to live with her as a roommate? Ridiculous! That is what Paul means. When she married, all those questions became out of order.

Now listen to Paul: "If ye be dead with Christ," and that is the situation when you are a believer in Christ, you are dead so far as this world is concerned. You are dead from the rudiments of the world. You are not related to the world any more in a direct way. You are insensitive to the things of the world. Then why do you make a lot of rules as though you were living in the world? "Touch not; taste not; handle not." You are out of it. Be through with it. Leave it alone. When a young man joins the Marines, do you think he will start figuring what kind of suit of clothes he will wear next fall? That is already settled.

Remember, Paul was arguing with his readers. He was trying to tell them that the rules and regulations by which people lead religious lives are not the way in which they would live the spiritual life. They would live the spiritual life by letting God work His will through them by His Holy Spirit. Thus they would have the life of Christ actually living in them. If they were dead with Christ from the rudiments of the world, so far as this world is concerned they had been crucified. Since they were crucified, they were finished with it. Since they were through with it, why should they set up a number of little rules to deal with it; the rules being "touch not, taste not, handle not." When they are in this situation they are no longer sensitive to things of this world. So why would they need rules, especially those made up by men?

I have been discussing what it means to be dead with Christ. I noted in a previous chapter how a dead body has ears, but the auditory nerve in the ear does not respond. A dead body has eyes, but the light that shines through the eyelids into the eyeballs does not stimulate the optic nerve because it is dead. Inasmuch as believers are dead with Christ, and this world does not appeal to them any more, they are through with it. They do not need to set up a lot of little rules. The apostle Paul said to believers in Christ that rules and regulations are not what is needed in spiritual experience. What is needed is fellowship with the Lord. The Lord Himself will be in them and He is minded to do the right thing. Rules and regulations are made up by men, and Christ is far beyond them. He is actually in the presence of His Father, doing what is pleasing in the Father's sight. So we can understand that if a believer is truly obedient to Christ he will not need rules and regulations that are made up by men.

A FORM OF GODLINESS
(Colossians 2:23)

Do you realize that being religious does not necessarily mean the person belongs to Christ?

> Which things have indeed a show of wisdom in will-worship, and humility, and neglecting of the body; not in any honor to the satisfying of the flesh (Col. 2:23).

One of the difficulties we have about understanding this part of the Scriptures (and I think the apostle Paul felt it when he wrote this epistle) is that there are so many people outside the church who feel competent to tell anybody what a real believer in Christ would be like, even though they do not understand what it is all about. I suspect that in any given situation, if you were present with six other people, at least three of them would feel sure they could tell you what a believer in Christ really is, even though they are not believers themselves. There seem to be some who think that being a believer in Christ means that you attend church. They may have in mind that some day they will start attending church services. Usually they are the kind who show up when the meeting begins and they stay until the meeting closes; then they go home and mark down that they have been to church one more time. I went to church many times as a boy and afterwards as a young man when I was not a believer; I even went to church when I was an agnostic.

Some people think that anybody who reads the Bible is a believer in Christ, so they start reading the Bible. I read the Bible when I was an unbeliever. Any number of unbelievers read the Bible. Sometimes people get interested in it, sometimes they argue about it. Sometimes they are actually against it, but they read it to find mistakes in it. And there are some people who read the Bible because they think it is some kind of virtue. They think if they read one chapter it is good; two chapters are twice as good; three chapters, three times as good, and so on. These people read the Bible as a kind of rule to make themselves good.

I have nothing against reading the Bible, but that is not what will make you good. Some people feel that way about prayer. They feel that if you just pray you will be good; if you just pray you will be a believer in Christ. So they pray. There is nothing wrong with prayer, but prayer is not what makes you a believer in Christ. A person can have a cultivated humility. Some of the most humble people I have known were the biggest crooks in business. But humility served their purpose.

Some will deny the body. They will adopt strict rules of conduct, yet that does not necessarily make them believers in Christ. Not one of these actions is bad, but none is good enough to make one a believer in Christ.

Some years ago a Hindu traveled all over this country, attracting much attention. He was a very famous figure. There were people who called him "the greatest Christian" they ever knew. This man had read about Jesus Christ and did not believe in Him, yet many preachers said about him that he was a great "Christian." Actually he did deny his body. He walked around wrapped in a bedsheet; he did not drink coffee; and he carried his own special food along with him. Any number of people were ready to say he was a great "Christian."

Sometimes we can see this same thing in our churches. I often think that when I look at our big cathedral-like buildings with stained glass windows, when I hear soft and sweet music and the unctuous tones of a cultured man in the pulpit, it does not mean Christ is being worshiped. A person can worship Christ in a cave or a barn. You do not need "things" to worship Christ. Nowhere else in the New Testament is it expressed so plainly as here in the 23rd verse. This means making up your mind to worship God whether you feel like it or not. You are just going to do it.

"And humility." Some persons really do have an induced, voluntary humility. "And neglecting of the body." They put themselves under a strict regime. We know people who are not committed to Christ who will not drink coffee because it stimulates them too much, nor will they eat certain kinds of meat. "Not in any honor to the satisfying of the flesh." Paul is affirming that these things do not make a believer in Christ. Once, in a foreign country, I saw poor people on hands and knees crawling across a big plaza to get into a great cathedral. This was not really necessary. We know we can bow our hearts before God at any time and find Him. There is a group of people called the Penitents who beat themselves, especially around Easter, trying to make themselves like Christ Jesus. But we do not accept such procedure as true to the gospel.

These things are difficult to evaluate, I know. Not any one of them is comfortable to the human being, and not one is indulgent to the flesh; but they do not make a person more of a believer. They do not even make him a believer in Christ at all. There is no human effort of any kind that is of help to the spiritual life. What the soul needs to do is to look to Christ and have fellowship with Him. The believer has everything given to him as a gift. Blessing does not have to be earned, just received.

CHAPTER 3

† † †

SELF-DENIAL
(Colossians 3:1–3)

Do you know what a believer in Christ can do that will make it easy for him to live the spiritual life?

> If ye then be risen with Christ, seek those things which are above, where Christ sitteth on the right hand of God. Set your affection on things above, not on things on the earth. For ye are dead, and your life is hid with Christ in God (Col 3:1–3).

All believers in Christ live in touch with two worlds: this world, which is the world of sense, dealing with the things that you can hear, taste and touch; and the other world, the world of the Spirit, which is invisible. The believer in Christ will have points at which he touches this world and this world touches him. There will be involvement, and this arouses interest. Desires develop and values are felt and seen. It is often the case that in order to respond to the will of God the believer in Christ must deny the flesh. This is well nigh impossible if left to himself.

In order for me to be able to deny this world, I need help. It is almost impossible for a person to turn away from the things of this world because of the strength of the attachment; yet it is essential that the things of the flesh be denied. This is the only possible way the believer can walk with Christ Jesus. "If any man will be my disciple, let him deny himself" (Matt. 16:24).

In Colossians 3:1–2, Paul gives an exhortation, directing attention to what the believer can do. "If ye then be risen with Christ," (this "if" is not a matter of doubt or a way of expressing a question mark, this is a way of expressing a condition) "seek those things which are above, where Christ sitteth on the right hand of God." Let us keep in mind, believers are risen with Christ in the sense that, so far as this world is concerned, they have reckoned themselves dead. As they are dead with Christ from the rudiments of the world, so they are alive in Christ as far as the spiritual world is concerned. Since they are then risen with Christ in the resurrection, and actually have a life that is being lived in a spiritual relationship with God, Paul urges, "Set your affection on things above, not on things of the earth (away from this world) where Christ sitteth on the right hand of God."

What sort of things would those be which are above? Even as you are riding in your car, working in your home, what would those things be? Among other things there would be righteousness: being right in the sight of God. That is something that is above this world: something one finds in relationship with God. The joy of the Lord is something one does not get out of this world. One gets that in fellowship with God. Peace with God, the peace that passeth all understanding, is from above "where Christ sitteth on the right hand of God." It is not of this world. These are eternal things, where everything is done God's way.

"Set your affection on things above." These words are familiar to us, yet I think we sometimes have difficulty in understanding them. How can one set his affection on things above? An incident in my early life comes to my mind. I knew I intended to devote my life to fulltime service of the Lord and expected to go as a foreign missionary. I taught school in a country community in northern Manitoba and played baseball on the senior team in the community. The team was financed with money raised through special affairs: a concert, a debate, a box social and a dance. I did not dance at that time (this was part of my Christian testimony) although I took part in the debate. The team bought uniforms with part of the money raised. A question arose in my heart: should I wear a uniform and play in it, when the uniform was paid for with money made at a dance? The more I thought about it the more difficulty I had. I talked to my manager who encouraged me to go ahead and use the uniform, but still I was undecided. While praying and reading in the New Testament, this came to my heart, "Set your affection on things above." I knew baseball was not from above. I loved to play ball but my answer came in this fashion. I often think of this experience when I read this verse.

If we would set our affections on things above we would be free from many hindrances.

THE SECRET
(Colossians 3:3–4)

Do you know the secret of spiritual living?

> For ye are dead, and your life is hid with Christ in God. When Christ, who is our life, shall appear, then shall ye also appear with him in glory (Col. 3:3–4).

In this passage, Paul is pointing out to the Colossians that there is a heavenly dimension to spiritual experience. The believer in Christ lives in this world, surrounded by the things of this world, but there is no roof over him. Heaven is real, and he is right in the very presence of God. To understand a believer in Christ it is necessary to remember that there are two worlds. There is this present world in which we live as human beings, and there is the spiritual world, sometimes called the world to come. This first world we can call the world of sense in which we hear, see, taste, smell and touch the things you can hold in your hands. All human values are here in this present world. Then there is also the spiritual world where God is.

The basic fact of our spiritual life, of living the life of a believer in Christ, is that the resurrection of the Lord Jesus Christ has translated believers out of this world into the other world. I was born once of earthly parents. When I heard about what the Lord Jesus Christ had done, I was brought to believe in Jesus as the Christ and to receive Him as my Savior. Thus I was crucified with Christ and I was reckoned dead. A new life was begun in me, and this newness of life was the life of God in me through His Word. This was the eternal life that God promised, and thus I became a new creature. All of this was done by God by His grace through the gospel of the Lord Jesus Christ.

We read in verses 3 and 4, "For ye are dead, and your life is hid with Christ in God. When Christ, who is our life, shall appear, then shall ye also appear with him in glory." This is the real secret of spiritual life. When you reckon yourself dead, this world no longer has a grip on you. You are not involved in it. You are alive in Christ Jesus. There is something new working in you: the life of God in your soul.

In his first epistle the apostle John wrote, "Beloved, now are we the sons of God, and it doth not yet appear what we shall be: but we know that, when he shall appear, we shall be like him; for we shall see him as he is" (1 John 3:2). Believers have a human shell, but inwardly they are creatures in Christ Jesus. Paul expresses it in this way, "When Christ, who is our life [right now He is operative in us] shall appear, then shall ye also appear with him in glory." This word "appear" means when He is revealed, when He is openly manifested. Believers will be seen with Him in glory. This phrase "in glory" does not necessarily point to some place far away from this planet. The word "glory" rather refers to the state and condition of fulfillment; that is, in harvesttime when the job is done in the believer and he will appear with Christ completely made over. It is the prospect and the future destiny of all believers that they will be in the presence of God without spot and wrinkle, like the Lord Jesus Christ. That is what God has predestined for them. When Christ appears, believers are to be with Him in glory. "It doth not yet appear what we shall be: but we know that when he shall appear, we shall be like him." That they are to be revealed with Christ Jesus is their expectation, and thus they can be strengthened to turn away from the things of this world.

If a person is a believer in the Lord Jesus Christ there is something true about him that the world would never guess. The apostle John said, "Therefore the world knoweth us not, because it knew him not." The world did not recognize Jesus of Nazareth as the Son of God, and the world will not recognize the believer as a child of God; but God looks down on him with mercy and compassion and grace. Are you a believer in the Lord Jesus Christ? If so, it can be said about you as it was of the apostle Paul, "I am crucified with Christ: nevertheless I live; yet not I, but Christ liveth in me: and the life which I now live in the flesh I live by the faith of the Son of God, who loved me, and gave himself for me" (Gal. 2:20).

So far as this world is concerned, a believer in Christ does not need it. He is going to leave it anyway. His life is dead with Christ Jesus and he actually belongs to God in Christ Jesus. The life of Christ is in him like a fountain. Eternal life shows up in him like water coming out of a spring in the mountains. He does not know where the water comes from, it just appears: and that is the way it is with the life in you. The believer has in him something that turns him to God; that moves him into God's will. If he but follows, it will make him do good to all men. His life is hid with Christ in God. It will really be revealed when Christ comes again. Then shall the believer also appear with Him in glory. Because this is true the believer can live a spiritual life. He can turn away from the things of this world to the things of the Lord Jesus Christ, because that is where he belongs.

RECKON YOURSELF DEAD
(Colossians 3:5–7)

Do you think if a person wants to be a real believer in Christ he needs to do anything about his former bad habits?

> Mortify therefore your members which are upon the earth; fornication, uncleanness, inordinate affection, evil concupiscence, and covetousness, which is idolatry: for which things' sake the wrath of God cometh on the children of disobedience: in the which ye also walked some time, when ye lived in them (Col. 3:5–7).

The mortician is one we call the undertaker, the person who takes the dead body and prepares it for burial. When we say "mortify" we are referring to doing something with the body that is dead. Perhaps I should coin a new English word, such as "deadify," "make dead," meaning you want to "count it dead." This is done by faith: by the inward attitude in which you count it as if it were dead. Scripture says of God in one place, "calling those things which be not, as though they were." Thus the believer speaks of his body and thinks of his body as if it were dead.

Notice that when Paul says "Mortify therefore your members which are upon the earth," he then mentions fornication and uncleanness. He does not mean that fornication, uncleanness or inordinate affection are members; rather "your members" have to do with your whole body—head, eyes, nose, mouth, ears, hands and all organs. If you reckon your members dead, fornication, uncleanness and inordinate affection will be out; also evil concupiscence and covetousness. In other words, fornication is something in which several members are involved. Uncleanness can involve all of your members. Inordinate affection and evil concupiscence may involve any of your members and covetousness will also involve any or all of your members. The members refer to your body here upon the earth, as you share in your environment in this world. These are "reckoned to be dead" if you "mortify" them.

A believer in Christ has members here on earth. He also has members in heaven. The members here in this world, his human nature, can lead him astray in response to the world found about him. So Paul exhorts him to count this human nature as if it were dead; then the following things will not be there: fornication, which is an indulgence of the flesh; uncleanness, which I think of as being selfish—when self is not denied; inordinate affection, an interest that is unreasonable, as when one cares too much about money or about pleasure, too much about your house or your position in the community. Evil concupiscence is an interest in things that are not proper, that are evil; and covetousness is idolatry.

Commonly speaking, there are few of us who pause long enough to understand what Paul is suggesting when he says that covetousness is idolatry. Of course, idolatry is the general term given to one's attitude toward an idol, which is anything that absorbs your time and your attention apart from God. Now, God can absorb your time, attention, and money, and that is clean. "Thou shalt love the LORD thy God with all thine heart, and with all thy soul, and with all thy might" (Deut. 6:5). That takes in everything, and that is clean. But when you give your time, thought, and money to something less than God, this is idolatry. That can be money, people, a position in the community, or anything else you may think more of than you do of God. When you are not content with such things as you have and reach out for other things, that is covetousness.

These things about which we have been thinking—fornication, uncleanness, inordinate affection, evil concupiscence, and covetousness—are all things which originate in yourself, in your body, when the members which are upon the earth are alive to the things of the world so that you desire them, "for which things' sake" (the development of these particular activities and attitudes in your heart) "the wrath of God cometh on the children of disobedience." The phrase "the wrath of God" should not be thought of as meaning only that God was angered. In verses 24, 26 and 28 in the first chapter of Romans you will find what God does in His wrath. When He brings the evil results of an evil deed upon the sinner, when He lets the wrong done actually produce wrong results: that is the wrath of God. The sad results that come from doing evil: that is the wrath of God. God will allow the sad results of doing evil to come upon the children of disobedience if they engage in fornication, uncleanness, inordinate affection, evil concupiscence, and covetousness. In order not to engage in these things, Paul urged, "mortify your members, reckon yourself dead."

Paul went on to say with reference to these attitudes or activities, "In the which ye also walked some time, when ye lived in them." The believer in Christ who wants to be truly spiritual can do something with reference to himself: he can reckon himself dead.

FREE FROM SIN
(Colossians 3:8–9)

If we say a believer in Christ is really free, do we mean he can do anything he feels like doing?

> But now ye also put off all these; anger, wrath, malice, blasphemy, filthy communication out of your mouth. Lie not one to another, seeing that ye have put off the old man with his deeds (Col. 3:8–9).

You can be a real believer in Christ and still have something of the flesh in you. To be a believer in Christ means that the soul has a certain conscious relationship with Jesus Christ. We do not start out that way. We are born the first time of the flesh. This is not necessarily sinister or evil: there is good flesh and bad flesh; but whatever the flesh is, it is not that in which you can enter the kingdom of God. "Flesh and blood cannot inherit the kingdom of God" (1 Cor. 15:50). When you are born again, regenerated, you receive Christ and become a child of God. These are various ways of referring to what happens when the soul accepts Jesus Christ. When that happens the individual is a babe in Christ, and he can then look forward to growing into maturity.

Peter wrote, "As newborn babes, desire the sincere milk of the word, that ye may grow thereby" (1 Peter 2:2). Thus the young believer who is a babe in Christ has the flesh with which he was born as a human being, and the spirit with which he was born again. Now flesh is flesh, no matter where and when you find it. It has a proclivity to evil. The flesh is called "the old man," while the spirit is called "the new man." So the believer in Christ has in him flesh, which refers to his human origin, and spirit, which refers to his origin from God. In the book of Galatians it is written that the flesh and the spirit are contrary one to the other, and they are both in every believer.

The believer in Christ can do something against the flesh, and he can do something for the spirit. He can "put off" the flesh, and he can "put on" the spirit. This is what is emphasized here in Colossians. As a person grows in Christ there is less of the flesh and more of the spirit. Paul exhorts believers to work with this growing process. This can be accomplished with a certain attitude toward the flesh and toward the spirit. The attitude toward the flesh should be that the believer will put it off, get rid of it. So we read, "But now ye also put off all these." This refers to a number of overt acts. Remember how we noted in our last study, "Mortify therefore your members which are upon the earth." Fornication, uncleanness, inordinate affection, evil concupiscence, and covetousness are all based upon inner attitudes of the desires. But now, in verses 7–9 the emphasis is on overt acts, outward practices. "Anger, wrath and malice" these are in conduct. "Blasphemy" is in speech and in the attitude of mind. "Filthy communication out of your mouth" is something a person says. "Lie not one to another" is something that you say. All these activities are carried on outwardly. It is possible to take a positive attitude of repudiation toward these. A person can have habits of anger and wrath that he can check; he can have a disposition toward malice that can be stopped. A person can have a habit of blasphemy that he can quit, and a way of producing filthy communication out of his mouth that he can stop. Persons do not have to lie one to another.

Let us now look more closely at each of these words. "Anger": to feel anger is not necessarily sin. You will find in the Gospels that on occasion Jesus of Nazareth experienced anger. We know He was without sin, yet on occasion He looked with anger in His heart upon certain persons. However, anger has a proclivity toward sin. When a person feels angry it should be curtailed. A person should not stay mad: "Let not the sun go down upon your wrath" (Eph. 4:26). Anger is the feeling you have of resentment and of potential conflict, but wrath deals with people according to their deeds. Wrath is what you do when in your heart and mind you have become angry with someone and you plan to get even because of what they have done to you. Malice is a carry-over of wrath, so that when you have an opportune time you can unload on them. Blasphemy is something you think or say with reference to God. It is irreverence toward God.

Filthy communications out of your mouth is a matter of suggestive comments that could stir up wrong responses. This word "filthy" brings to mind such things as personal conduct that is filthy, immorality of one sort or another. But that is not necessarily what is referred to here. Whenever you see the word "filthy" in a situation like this, you need to think of the spiritual significance of these terms. The spiritual significance of filthy communications out of your mouth suggests communications that stir wrong responses: communication you would have about something that is not right. The things you say with your mouth stir up evil conduct, and that makes it filthy communication.

"Lie not one to another" is a general call for integrity and truthfulness. Lying is what you do to each other when you misrepresent things.

The believer in Christ has a responsibility about what he allows his "old man" to do or to suggest. He has in him tendencies to anger and to wrath, to malice and to blasphemy, to saying things that stir wrong responses and to lying. He is not to allow these things to run rampant. So we say, "If a person is really a believer in the Lord Jesus Christ, does that mean he can do anything he feels like doing?" No. Because he may have in him something of the old man. There may be in him something that is entirely human. The human element in him will feel anger and wrath and malice. The human element may think wrong things about God, and actually intimate and say things that are wrong to other people because we are not perfect persons. We have these imperfections in us but the believer in Christ has a positive attitude about those things. His positive attitude is that he will put these things off. This means that he can actually do something about it. He can eliminate or control these things. He should do so and put them off because of the Spirit of Christ which is in him.

NEVER THE SAME
(Colossians 3:10–11)

Do you realize that when a person becomes a believer in Christ he starts to become an entirely different person?

> And have put on the new man, which is renewed in knowledge after the image of him that created him: where there is neither Greek nor Jew, circumcision nor uncircumcision, Barbarian, Scythian, bond nor free: but Christ is all, and in all (Col. 3:10–11).

In these words the apostle Paul indicated to the believers in Christ at Colossae what was involved in becoming believers and what there was for them to do. Paul emphasized what can happen, what should happen, and what does happen to the believer. Becoming a believer in Christ is a matter of becoming a special kind of person from the inside. No one is born with a personality. We know that a child born to the Smith family will begin to act like the Smiths, and a child born in the Jones home is likely to do something which will fit in with the plan of the Joneses. That does not mean that when the baby was born he had these characteristics, but when he grew up as a child he acquired them. He developed them in the social group to which he belonged.

Becoming a believer in Christ is not a matter of educating a man in a better way of living, or training him to do things differently. There would be nothing wrong with this approach (namely, teaching a man what to do and urging him to do it) except that it would not work.

Paul writes in one place, "For what the law could not do, in that it was weak through the flesh, God sending his own Son in the likeness of sinful flesh, and for sin, condemned sin in the flesh" (Rom. 8:3). The law will tell you what to do. Now the law can tell you the right thing to do, and if you would do it, it would be right; but the fact is, as you hear about it, see it, and look ahead, it is not easy to identify the end at the beginning. The chances are that you will make your choice according to certain considerations you already have in mind.

Christ offers to "whosoever will" His personal presence and His Spirit to enable such to do the will of God through Him. When you believe in the Lord Jesus Christ, you do not face any choice alone. The Lord Jesus Himself will be with you. Those who accept Christ by the Word and the Spirit of God are born again. This is the real meaning of the word "renewed." Believers are renewed in knowledge after the image of Him that created them but not to be the same kind of person as before.

Paul refers in this epistle to the old man and the new man. We have been thinking about that. The old man was natural: just out of human nature. He was human and interested in himself. The new man is spiritual. He gets his ideas from the Spirit of God; he is of God instead of being of man, and he is interested in Christ and in heaven. The new man who has these attributes is renewed. That is to say, he is made new. His very habits of life are made new by the grace of God. He is fed by knowledge; and knowledge, as you know, is a matter of the consciousness—the conscious recognition of all that is. The more truth you know, the better it will be for you. This new man is shaped up to be like Jesus of Nazareth, the Son of God.

Since human considerations no longer matter, when the believer is like the Son of God, he will think in terms of the things of heaven and the things of God. Human considerations do not enter in, and because of that no attention is paid to human judgment. This means no distinctions in the new man, in Christ Jesus, with reference to common human distinctions. Paul lists a number of them: "Where there is neither Greek nor Jew." There is neither Greek nor Jew in the new man because there is neither Greek nor Jew in Christ Jesus. Christ Jesus is the Son of God. He is not the son of a Greek or the son of a Jew.

The believer in Christ is the son of God, and as such he has everything from God. So, "there is neither Greek nor Jew, circumcision nor uncircumcision." When once a person is born again in Christ Jesus, it does not matter whether he was dedicated to Christ as a child, or whether he was not dedicated to Christ as a child. There is neither "Barbarian, Scythian, bond nor free." "Neither bond nor free" means there is no such thing as a slave, nor such a thing as a master, so far as the believer in Christ is concerned.

What is meant by all this? In this world there are Greeks and there are Jews; there are people who are circumcised and there are people who are uncircumcised. There are those who are called Barbarians and Scythians, and there are people who are slaves and people who are free from slavery. These human categories belong in this world, but they do not become the categories of the life of a believer in Christ. They are not meaningful to him as the new man, who is born of God by the Lord Jesus Christ.

I am impressed with the idea that in the New Testament the truth as it is shown to us is that Jesus of Nazareth never developed an "ego" as Jesus of Nazareth. I do not know that He ever referred to Himself as Jesus of Nazareth. So far as I know, the only time he called Himself "Jesus" was when Paul met Him on the Damascus Road. He was then already in heaven in the presence of God. "I am Jesus whom thou persecutest." While here on earth He referred to Himself as the Son of God, the Son of Man, and a Child of God. It is enough for us now to just have in mind that when a soul is in Christ, human distinctions fade away.

BE LIKE JESUS
(Colossians 3:12–13)

Is it clear to you that for a person to become a believer in Christ he must be willing to decide to be and to do as the Lord wants him to be and do?

> Put on therefore, as the elect of God, holy and beloved, bowels of mercies, kindness, humbleness of mind, meekness, long-suffering; forbearing one another, and forgiving one another, if any man have a quarrel against any: even as Christ forgave you, so also do ye (Col. 3:12–13).

Why did Jesus come? Few people know why Christ came. He did not come to make money or to run a government. He did not come to write books nor to paint pictures. He came to die for sinners. Not everybody understands that, and we should tell them.

While it seems plain that what takes place in a believer in Christ is what God does, it is also plain that what God does includes the quickening of the will of the believer. The developing of the spiritual life is not something that takes place automatically. You do not grow as a believer the way your muscles grow and the way your bones grow as your human body develops. There is an element of choice involved because of the grace of God that is operative. God affects my inner consciousness, and I will choose to do His will.

Let us look now at verses 12–13. "Put on therefore, as the elect of God" is an imperative. This is something that you can do, as one who is chosen of God. A better way of saying this would be "called out of the world to be with God" because they are called out of the flesh, out of nature, to be with God "holy and beloved." (The word "holy" refers to their personal attitude. It is a case of being totally committed to God, altogether His, with nothing of self.) "And beloved" refers to God's attitude toward us. We are the fortunate recipients of "bowels of mercies, kindness, humbleness of mind, meekness, long-suffering."

For a moment I want to look at this (for us) inelegant word "bowels." We do not ordinarily use this particular reference with regard to our body organs, yet it is used here; and this phrase reflects the terminology of the day. In the Old Testament, especially in poetry, the Hebrews, when they spoke about a man having certain pain, would speak of "a dart in his liver" (Prov. 7:23). Another organ the Hebrews referred to time and again is the kidneys. We do not find that word in the King James Version because they used the word "reins," but what was actually meant was kidneys. Sometimes Scriptures use the word "heart": "My heart is pained within me." All three of these organs, which are called the visceral organs, refer to something that is inside the body. The Greeks used the common word "bowels." This is a striking reference in what we call somatic consciousness (the sympathetic nervous system) to the visceral organs in different ways. Today, we still would not know which one of these organs to be specific about. Some people have emotions that affect their heart so that it starts beating rapidly; but others have other visceral organs disturbed in this way.

Paul wrote here that you are to adjust your thinking in such a way that you will adopt this sympathetic attitude, or emotional pattern. A heart of mercy, kindness, humbleness of mind, meekness and long-suffering indicates various aspects of a general frame of mind which has earnest concern for other people. Mercy will be extended to the person who is at a disadvantage. Kindness is the way you feel toward the person who is in need. Humbleness of mind is the way you feel about yourself compared to other people. Meekness is the word we are concerned with when someone has done you wrong: when you could retaliate with pleasure to get even but you do not do it. Long-suffering refers to a general attitude of heart in which you will not be stampeded into action "forbearing one another, and forgiving one another, if any man have a quarrel against any: even as Christ forgave you, so also do ye."

This entire description is a careful setting forth of the ways of Christ. You will remember that in our last study we noted that the new man is renewed in knowledge after the image of Him that created him. Now if the believer is renewed in knowledge he is renewed in his consciousness, in his thinking and his mind. He will be renewed after the image of Christ that created him. In these verses we have a description of that image. This whole passage is an exhortation that the elect of God, the people who are called of God, holy and beloved (holy in the sense they are entirely committed to God, beloved in the sense He really cares for them), are to put on this thing which would be the image of Christ. This is what the believer is to put on not only with lip service (just saying he is going to do it) but actually have it as his pattern of conduct. And here are some of the things he is to put before him. There is to be mercy, kindness, humbleness of mind, meekness, long-suffering, and forgiving one another. Each one has its own particular slant but the general idea all the way through is one of goodwill. Believers in Christ should really want to help people. "If any man have a quarrel against any: even as Christ forgave you, so also do ye." Because he loves them, he will give to them; he will be kind to them, humble in their presence, and he will be glad to have fellowship with them. Because he loves them he will be meek. In case they have done something that was wrong he will be long-suffering, forbearing in love and forgiving another as God for Christ's sake has forgiven him. This is what a believer can choose to do.

This description is not only something the Lord will impel the believer to, but something he can strive for.

THE BELIEVER'S ATTITUDE
(Colossians 3:14–15)

What is the general frame of mind a believer in Christ can adopt for his own blessing?

> And above all these things put on charity, which is the bond of perfectness. And let the peace of God rule in your hearts, to the which also ye are called in one body; and be ye thankful (Col. 3:14–15).

In these words the apostle Paul continues his exhortation to these believing people in Colossae as to what they should do to improve their spiritual experience in Christ. We find here exhortation to certain things that pertain to the frame of mind any believer should have. These are simple words, full of meaning to us. Let us look at them. "And above all these things [everything he has been saying, especially with reference to what believers are to put on] put on charity, which is the bond of perfectness." The bond of perfectness refers to a kind of belt that would be wrapped around everything else: the bond of completion. The perfectness of being everything you should be, competent and mature in spiritual matters.

Let us look again at the word "charity" or "loving kindness." The Greeks had a separate word for the kind of love that has to do with communion. It is "agape." But this word "charity" is used for anybody. *Charitas* is the way the Greeks would say it. It has in it an element of kindness and of helpfulness to all people, and it has no personal interest in getting any special returns.

"And let the peace of God rule in your hearts, to the which also ye are called in one body; and be ye thankful." As a believer in Christ you are to share in this peace of God. My attention has been called to the fact that this word "rule" as translated here could have been translated "umpire." "Let the peace of God umpire in your hearts." Let this be the inward experience you have about making decisions. What does an umpire do? He says this is right and that is wrong; he calls this person "safe" and that person "out." So when you have the peace of God ruling in your heart, you can rule this thing safe and that thing out, because it is the way the peace of God would cause you to feel.

The word "peace" refers to an inward quietness. The peace of God which He gives will be very sensitive to conflict because conflict would disturb it. This is the peace that comes to the believer when he is reconciled to God: when he is assured of God's presence and keeping power. This is the peace the believer has when he is in love with other people, and in his heart he wants to be at peace with them, and to be in fellowship with them. Let this peace umpire in you when you drive in city traffic. Keep a respectful distance from others, and if you see someone trying to get out of a lane and come into your lane, slow down and let them come. In your business, if you have strain and tension and are tempted to worry, remember the providence of God and put your trust in Him. Putting your trust in the Lord will promote the peace of God in your heart. With reference to the poor, sometimes the thought of them can disturb you. What should you do? Well, give to them and when you do, trust God, "and the peace of God, which passeth all understanding, shall keep your hearts and minds through Christ Jesus" (Phil. 4:7).

It is written in Philippians that whatever comes up, in everything, with prayer and supplication you should pray that your requests may be known unto God. And the peace of God will guard your heart and mind in Christ Jesus. You have been called into a fellowship with God where you can have peace. Certain things will contribute to that and certain things will disturb it. Those things that would disturb, call or rule them out, like an umpire.

"And be ye thankful." Being thankful will mean you will have a certain attitude toward God, knowing that every good thing comes from Him. He will watch over you in every way, every day. And in everything you will be thankful because God has done things for you. In this way you can have a frame of mind that will keep you in fellowship with the Lord, and you will be blessed with peace.

SING UNTO THE LORD
(Colossians 3:16–17)

Do you realize how important singing can be to your own spiritual experience as a believer in Christ?

> Let the word of Christ dwell in you richly in all wisdom; teaching and admonishing one another in psalms and hymns and spiritual songs, singing with grace in your hearts to the Lord. And whatsoever ye do in word or deed, do all in the name of the Lord Jesus, giving thanks to God and the Father by him (Col. 3:16–17).

In these words the apostle Paul is showing believers in Christ how they could live their spiritual lives in fullest measure of blessing. I wonder if you notice the change in the tone when he says in verse 16, "Let the word of Christ dwell in you richly." It began in verse 15, "And let the peace of God rule in your hearts." From the first verse in this chapter the imperatives have been in active voice. For instance, "Seek those things which are above." That is something you can do. Also, "Set your affection on things above." That likewise is something you can do. Verse 5, "Mortify therefore your members":

that is for you to do when you reckon them to be dead. Verse 8, "Put off all these": that is something you can do. Verse 9, "Lie not one to another": that is your responsibility, the way you report things to each other. Verse 10, "Put on the new man": you can do that. Verse 12, "Put on therefor, as the elect of God." There follows another list of things you are to do. Verse 14, "And above all these things, put on charity." Each is a positive imperative.

Now in verses 15 and 16, Paul changes his tone altogether, "Let the peace of God rule." Do nothing about it; let it rule. Bring it to your mind and consciousness, and be aware of it; and let the Holy Spirit show you those things. They will affect your mind and the judgments you make. Verse 16, "Let the word of Christ dwell in you richly in all wisdom" is something that, in a sense, almost seems as though you are passive. But it is an aggressive God who is doing this for you. Both verses 15 and 16 are entirely in His will; He will do something. Let us look more closely at verse 16, "the word of Christ." He will speak to your heart. Keep in mind that this will be in terms of Scripture. Let those passages that deal with the truth of Christ abide in your heart; they will dwell in you richly in all wisdom.

"Teaching and admonishing one another in psalms and hymns and spiritual songs, singing with grace in your hearts to the Lord." This is part of your spiritual preparation and part of the spiritual opportunity you have. When he uses the phrase "in all wisdom," it can become more obvious to you if you will substitute "in all good common sense." That is what it means.

If you are letting the Bible rest in your heart and mind in all good common sense, you can open your Old Testament Scriptures and find that you are constantly conscious of the living God, living in His presence. Now let this truth dwell in you richly by the psalms that you sing. A song repeats a central idea over and over again, and because it is pleasant to the ear, it is not monotonous. The music makes it easier for you to listen and it can be brought to your mind more often. Many of the old hymns reflect the whole gospel of the Lord Jesus Christ; all the teaching of the Bible is to be found right in those hymns. "Singing with grace in your hearts to the Lord."

"And whatsoever ye do in word or deed, do all in the name

of the Lord Jesus, giving thanks to God and the Father by him." That covers everything you do and say. And you are to do all in the name of the Lord. I do not think that means you are to act and then say, "Well, this is for God's sake." As you act you will be thinking of Him, doing what would please Him. You do it all, trusting in Him. This is serving and praying in the name of the Lord.

One of the simplest ways you can operate under the name of another person is to be that person's child, because the child takes the name of the father. When you speak about doing things in the name of the Lord, you can ask yourself if you are born again. Another way in which a person uses the name of another is in a partnership when he can use the name of the firm, and sign the firm's name because he is a partner. And so it is with the Lord Jesus Christ. If you are partner in the work He is doing, you will find that the privilege of praying is open to you. The privilege of getting help from the Lord is open to you because you are operating in His name.

So being born again gives you the privilege of having the name of the Lord; being a member of the bride of Christ gives you the name of the Lord; being a partner with Him in service gives you the name of the Lord. And "whatsoever ye do in word or deed, do all in the name of the Lord Jesus, giving thanks to God and the Father by him." Remember that everything that happens, happens by the grace of God. You would not be able to do anything if God did not help you.

CHRIST IN THE HOME
(Colossians 3:18–19)

Are you aware that being a believer in Christ will affect your home?

> Wives, submit yourselves unto your own husbands, as it is fit in the Lord. Husbands, love your wives, and be not bitter against them (Col. 3:18–19).

It is natural to think of spiritual experience as related to God. When we think of being a believer in Christ in terms such as that of praying to God, worshiping Him, and witness-

ing to the Lord Jesus Christ, we think of the soul; we think of
heaven; we think of the Holy Spirit; we think of judgment and
all things that pertain to God. That is proper because, of
course, these are things with which we deal. Yet in our personal participation in the things of the Lord all of these have a
bearing upon the life we live here in this world. And that life
here is lived out in response to the living God Himself. Paul is
showing us here that when we let the Word of Christ dwell
richly in our hearts, every aspect of our lives will be affected.
He will now discuss a number of personal relationships in
which this will be seen.

"Wives, submit yourselves unto your own husbands, as it is
fit in the Lord. Husbands, love your wives, and be not bitter
against them." Here the apostle Paul brings into focus the
primary fellowship among human beings on earth, the mar-
riage relationship. Wives and husbands, there is a word from
the Lord for each of you, and you are to let this word dwell in
you richly. Let us see what is said first to wives. In verses
12–17 believers are to put on kindness, mercies, humbleness
of mind, meekness, long-suffering, forbearing one another,
forgiving one another, and charity. The peace of God is to
dwell in their hearts, they are to be thankful, they are to let
the word of Christ dwell in them richly in all good common
sense. Whatsoever they do in word or deed, they are to do all
in the name of the Lord, giving thanks to God.

With all of that in mind, wives should submit themselves
unto their own husbands. They are to yield the executive
leadership in their home to the husband. This may require
grace. There are times when a wife can see where her husband makes mistakes; he may actually do foolish things. He
may choose to travel a certain route and the wife may know it
is not a good route; it will be rough and perhaps dangerous,
but he is determined. She should submit herself. How can
she do it? By trusting in the Lord and accepting the Providence that brought the two together. Wives are to submit
themselves unto their own husbands. I do not think there is
anything particularly sinister about putting in the word
"own," but it is quite possible that every now and again a wife,
standing on the sidelines, may see some other man she thinks
would do the job better. She is asked, however, to submit

herself to her own husband "as it is fit in the Lord." This is the one place where she might have her biggest problem, where the demand for grace will be at its most crucial point. But she is to yield herself into the situation, accept it, and live in it.

"Husbands, love your wives, and be not bitter against them." That is all that is said. I can imagine someone saying that is no trouble because he is in love with his wife. That is wonderful. But I can think of some cases when the man would say, "Don't ask me to do that." But he *is* asked to do that. Let me draw your attention to this word "love," where it says "love your wives." Generally speaking, "love" as used in the New Testament is not a sentimental emotion. Many times a husband may have sentimental feelings toward his wife, and that is fine; but that is not what is being talked about here. In the book of Ephesians we read, "Husbands, love your wives, even as Christ also loved the church" (Eph. 5:25). As you think about that, you will know that Christ is not pleased with everything the church does. The church is not perfect in the sight of Christ. He could see all the faults and failings in the church. But what does it say? "As Christ also loved the church, and gave himself for it." That is the point. It is an action on your part. Love involves care and action. "As Christ loved the church." He was not approving it. He was not adoring, esteeming, or being sentimental about it. This is not the kind of love one has because the other person is lovely. It is the case where a man does for his wife because he is in a position to do for her; she needs help and so he gives it. An outstanding example of this kind of love is the story of Hosea and Gomer in the Old Testament. Hosea rescued his wife from a debauched life out of love for the unlovely.

"And be not bitter against them." You may wonder why that is brought in here. It refers to a very common emotional experience. It often happens that men get bitter toward the very women they live with. Sometimes I think a husband may have the feeling that a wife does not really appreciate what he is going through. He may have the feeling she does not realize how hard he works, because she may criticize what he has done when he has really done his best. But this husband is told not to be bitter toward his wife. He is to do for her as unto the Lord.

So both wives and husbands can find the full exercise of their spiritual living right in their own home. They can have confidence in the providence that brought them together, and they can depend upon the grace of God for strength. In each case there is something natural to overcome and something spiritual to receive.

PARENT-CHILD RELATIONSHIPS
(Colossians 3:20–21)

Have you any idea how a father can provoke his children to anger?

> Children, obey your parents in all things: for this is well-pleasing unto the Lord. Fathers, provoke not your children to anger, lest they be discouraged (Col. 3:20–21).

One of the reasons why the Bible is so important is because it tells us about God. The Bible will also tell you about the soul, and it will tell you about heaven. The Bible will tell you how to be forgiven. The Bible will also tell you how to have the presence of God, and what you need to do that you might have the blessing of God. Paul has been telling the believers in Christ at Colossae that if they walk with Christ they can be quite sure the Lord will make changes in them. They will actually see themselves being transformed.

Naturally speaking, they were the children of the flesh. Spiritually, they became children of God. It is the most natural thing in the world to be human; it is not natural to be a child of God. But it is possible through grace. So the apostle is urging them to learn more and more what it means to put away the things of the flesh, the things that are natural, and to receive the things that are spiritual, that belong to God. In doing this they are to expect to be changed from day to day.

In chapter 3 we were taught that there are some things we should put off, then we were taught that there are some things we should put on. We are instructed to put on an attitude of receiving everything from the Lord and doing everything unto the Lord. This brings us now to verses 20 and 21, "Children, obey your parents in all things: for this is well-pleasing unto the Lord." That is all that is said to children.

"Fathers, provoke not your children to anger, lest they be discouraged." When Paul just says that much and no more, what shall we think? That there is nothing else involved? We should not think that. When he says "children," he is referring to the fact that these human beings have parents, and here is the simple admonition with reference to parents. Children should obey them in all things. Someone may say that will cause problems. We should not be surprised about that. There are plenty of problems, but that does not change facts. The parents could be wrong sometimes. But sometimes they could be right. To be blessed and to follow through in the will of the Lord, the believing child will be obedient to the parents at all times, for this is well-pleasing unto the Lord. Should the child do what the parents want which may not be wise, God is able to overrule and bring blessing.

"Fathers, provoke not your children to anger, lest they be discouraged." I suspect there are some who are surprised that the Bible tells a man not to provoke his children to anger. If you ask how this can be avoided in discipline, the fact is that no child will ever really get mad because of discipline. Children brought up in homes where there is discipline do not develop hatred for their parents. What children cannot accept is for their parents to be inconsistent. If the father requires faithfulness in the children while he is not faithful, it is enough to make a boy angry. If a father demands that the child go to Sunday school and church while the father does not go, that can make the child angry. Another thing, if parents are prone to find fault and never recognize anything good about the children, that also is provoking.

In all these things you will note that the social processes that go on in the home between children and parents are natural. But the dynamic, the inward impulse to do right comes from the Lord.

WHO IS A SERVANT?
(Colossians 3:22–25)

Did you know that a servant who is a believer in Christ can live his life in such a way as to be richly blessed of God?

> Servants, obey in all things your masters according to the flesh; not with eye-service, as menpleasers; but in singleness of heart, fearing God: and whatsoever ye do, do it heartily, as to the Lord, and not unto men; knowing that of the Lord ye shall receive the reward of the inheritance: for ye serve the Lord Christ. But he that doeth wrong shall receive for the wrong which he hath done: and there is no respect of persons (Col. 3:22–25).

It is a common understanding that the gospel of Christ is directed to the poor and to the needy. We all rejoice in that because it is true. The Lord Jesus Himself said that "the poor have the gospel preached unto them." But I wonder how many of us realize that there is no promise in the New Testament that the poor will become rich, or that the needy will become independent. In our day much is being made of the idea that it is a spiritual duty to help the poor. I am sure that will always be acceptable to the Lord, but those who talk about this in public tie it up with the idea that we should help these people not to be poor. I am sure that if it were possible to do so, it would be all right; but this is not what the gospel actually teaches. I am sure the gospel has no particular interest in keeping anybody poor, but it does not promise that the time will come when there will be no poor people. As a matter of fact, the New Testament has told us in the words of the Lord Jesus, "the poor you have always with you" (Matt. 26:11).

Many turn to the New Testament for inspiration and guidance on how to deal with problems of labor, but seldom do we hear just what the New Testament actually says to those who labor. Our study deals with the question in verses 22 to 25, an exhortation Paul wrote with reference to servants. He is not writing this as a principle of spiritual living. Some believers in Christ are servants. There is a sense in which all of us who accept responsibility can count ourselves servants. Thus we will find that this passage applies to us.

Let us think now of those who work for somebody else. This is what we find. "Obey in all things your masters according to the flesh." I am quite sure that what Paul has in mind is your service. It is conceivable the servant might have parts of his life that will not be spent on the job, but so far as his relationship with the job is concerned he is to act according to the instructions his master gives him. "Your masters according to the flesh [your human bosses] not with eye-service, as menpleasers [this expression "eye-service" is probably self-explanatory: not doing things only to be seen so that they look all right, as if you were just trying to please men], but in singleness of heart."

"Singleness of heart" means sincerity, genuineness, fearing God. This is a way of saying, "Do not try to get by with an inferior performance, something that is superficial. Just do the very best you can with God as your Judge." This is the first word that is spoken to servants. It is not telling them what they will get or for what they are to pray. It is telling them as servants what they are to do. Believers in Christ depend on God to take care of them. They want to be well-pleasing in His sight; therefore, they are to carry out whatever instructions are given to them on their job as if they were doing for God Himself.

"And whatsoever ye do, do it heartily, as to the Lord, and not unto men." That is the word spoken to believing laborers. "Knowing that of the Lord ye shall receive the reward of the inheritance: for ye serve the Lord Christ." All the time the servant works he is not thinking of wages, he is thinking of what God sees him doing and of how God will bless him with the inheritance of the Lord Christ. For God will bless whosoever is faithful in Christ Jesus. When the laborer makes his ordinary daily work something wherein he can actually have personal dealings and fellowship with his Lord, serving Him right while he is doing his work, this will change the whole outlook so far as labor is concerned. "But he that doeth wrong shall receive for the wrong which he hath done." God will deal with everybody, everywhere, who, in relationship with other people, doesn't play it fair and square. If the servant does wrong to others, he can expect that wrong will be done to him.

I would not say this is the only principle operative in service or that this makes it possible to predict exactly what the Lord will do, but there is one thing we can know: if we do the things the Lord wants us to do, He will favor us. If we do the things the Lord does not want us to do, He will oppose us now and in the future. Everything we do, our personal integrity in our work and our dependability, is subject to the judgment of Almighty God. He will not condone anything that is evil or out of line. It is important for servants to remember that they are expected to do honestly and faithfully what they are called upon to do so that they might be blessed in the Lord.

CHAPTER 4

† † †

MANAGEMENT AND LABOR
(Colossians 4:1)

Did you know that God is especially interested in the way an employer deals with his employees?

> Masters, give unto your servants that which is just and equal;
> knowing that ye also have a Master in heaven (Col. 4:1).

Paul has been dealing with different groups: he has spoken to wives and then to husbands, children and then to fathers. He has spoken to servants. Now He speaks to masters. When Paul speaks of "masters" he is speaking of employers. Circumstances change but the relationship of the employer and the employee is universal. In the world of work and industry there has always been the master and the servant; the employer and the employee. Nothing in the Bible hints that this will ever be changed, but there are principles that can help deal with problems that arise.

"Masters, give unto your servants that which is just and equal." Masters should see to it that their servants get just and equal pay. Consider those words "just" and "equal" for a moment. Masters are to see to it that their servants get pay that is fair. They are not to get too much or too little. It is to be fair. There is to be justice in the handling of these matters. We know, of course, that wages are not going to be always the same. The next word is "equal," but equal does not refer to the amount, as we shall see. You may live under conditions where a certain amount of money is paid per hour, whether the man works or does not work; just so he is on the job. We may have to accept that from the standpoint of management and labor, but that is not scriptural. It was never intended to work out that way.

The problem of wages has always been the classic problem so far as labor is concerned. These two qualifications are basic to the whole discussion: fair and just, no advantage either way. It is the responsibility of the employer to see that this is done. The servant cannot always know. He will often think he is entitled to more money when the circumstances are such that if we gave him more it would be unfair. He could be getting more than the master gets. The servant is not in a position to know, but the master is. He knows what the overhead is and can understand it. He is to do what is fair.

The New Testament has something to say about management, labor, and capital, but what it has to say, people often do not want to hear. Scripture says, for example, that people should be treated fairly and equally. This equity is to be in distribution, not in the absolute amount. The problem of keeping wages equal can be seen when one man who works for an hour is compared to another man who works for an hour. The two jobs may be entirely different. One job may be very demanding and exhausting, the other may be fairly easy. Some men do work that is of such a nature that it injures their health. In such cases the master should by no means stick to the minimum wage.

There are other occasions when people will demand full wages for doing little work. If we had the New Testament pattern (which we do not have), we would see that this would require equity: the man who worked hard would be given more than the man who did little and worked slowly. It has become the custom that the amount of time a man puts in is counted as what he sells. So he sells his time. Thus we can have an equal rate so far as the time is concerned. I am not anxious to comment here upon contemporary economics and practices, except to say that the believer's attitude toward the whole business is that he will try to do the just and fair thing; he will aim at equity in distribution of wages.

"Knowing that ye also have a Master in heaven." Apparently the Lord in heaven watches to see how things are done. It is difficult for this to be applied in a large corporation where everything is completely structured and where there is collective bargaining. But in the handling of this matter in one's own personal affairs, with perhaps one or two servants, this can offer guidance to the believer. He is to do the thing that is fair, just and equal, "knowing that ye also have a Master in heaven." James says that the cry of the laborer goes up to God and God hears it. In the case James noted, a man did not pay his laborer at the end of the day and let him go through the night hungry and cold. God would notice that.

There are people today who make all kinds of rules and regulations that have to be kept meticulously. If any are broken, the pay will be held up regardless of what the consequence will be. That, also, is not good.

So here we have the pattern of the New Testament labor principle. The social message of the New Testament or the social implications of the gospel of Christ are very simple: the employee is to do the very best he can, and the employer is to be fair, honest, genuine, and play no favorites. Labor then will render a good job, and capital will pay fair wages. This is not a modern idea: it was all set forth in the Scriptures. For believers in Christ this is grounded in the grace of God. It is for believers dealing with men everywhere. If the believer in Christ is working for someone else, he will work as if he were working for the Lord and act accordingly. Someone working for the believer will be dealt with as if the money was being paid to Christ Himself. All this would be a blessing to those involved, and it is part of the blessing we have in Christ.

CONTINUE IN PRAYER
(Colossians 4:2–4)

Do you think a person should keep on praying again and again for the same thing?

> Continue in prayer, and watch in the same with thanksgiving; withal praying also for us, that God would open unto us a door of utterance, to speak the mystery of Christ, for which I am also in bonds: that I may make it manifest, as I ought to speak (Col. 4:2–4).

This passage does not so much stress reiterating requests, asking for the same things over and over, as it does emphasize that we should always be in the mood to seek God's way as we act. We should always be alert to note answers to prayers and to seek favor for the specific things we do. Praying is to the soul like breathing is to the body. In prayer we face God. We need to focus our attention upon God consciously and address our hearts and minds to Him. It strengthens us inwardly. Our human consciousness is made aware of God as we pray because we turn to Him as spiritual persons. In our spiritual experience our living is grounded in our believing. We live as we believe, but our believing is based upon what we have heard and what we remember about the invisible God. We can only believe such things as we are conscious of about God.

So the procedure seems to be something like this: the truth of God is revealed in His Word. We read the Bible and find out about Him. The truth of God is seen in His acts. We can look about us in providence and look back over the history of our lives and see the hand of God dealing with us in our affairs. The truth of God is revealed in our hearts by His Spirit because by His Holy Spirit He makes us conscious of the things that pertain to God. When we pray we are conscious of God and recall the things we have learned about Him.

Prayer normally has several aspects. First, there is some form of adoration. We think of something true about God that brings forth our praise: He is almighty, He is eternal, everlasting, gracious, kind and merciful. He will receive sinners; He will forgive sin. Then there is thanksgiving in which we thank God for things He has done. The familiar hymn goes, "Count your blessings, name them one by one, and it will surprise you what the Lord has done." If you want spiritual blessing, thank God for something He has done for you within the past twenty-four hours. After we have praised Him for who He is and thanked Him for what He has done for us, we bring our petitions. When we bring our needs before Him, we will call to mind the promises of God.

Notice what this verse goes on to say, "Continue in prayer, and watch in the same with thanksgiving." What does it mean to pray and watch? There is another place in Scripture where the phrase reads, "Watch and pray." Look about and see the need, and when you see the need, pray to God about it. Here the accent is somewhat different. Pray to God out of your heart and "watch thereunto." Watch and see what happens: keep an eye on the results and see whether or not anything will occur.

It is helpful to note answers to prayer because it will strengthen the believer. "Withal praying also for us, that God would open unto us a door of utterance." Paul asked them to remember him and to pray for him. God is minded to bless and He is willing to bless, but He will do more when you pray. "I will yet for this be inquired of by the house of Israel, to do it for them" (Ezek. 36:37). Paul requested prayer for providential opportunities. He wanted the privilege to preach. This is what we have in mind: we want to make known to people the truth of the gospel.

TODAY IS THE DAY
(Colossians 4:5)

Do you think there is any hurry or urgency about getting the gospel message to people?

> Walk in wisdom toward them that are without, redeeming the time (Col. 4:5).

It is important to pray now! Why all this urgency? I will tell you why. This is the only time you will ever get anything done. If God is going to save, He will do it whenever He sees fit. Such a thought is not good enough. When we think like that, we forget that the Bible has already said, "Today is the day of salvation" (2 Cor. 6:2). Now is the accepted time. If you want to do God's will, today is the day to do it.

Paul says, "Walk in wisdom toward them that are without, redeeming the time." Paul is saying in effect, "act with good common sense." "Walk" is like the word "act," and "wisdom" would be "good common sense." So act with good common sense in the sight of those who are not believers. Look at the last phrase, "redeeming the time." Other translations give a variety of treatments of that phrase, but the general thought is always the same. Here is a good translation: "buying up the opportunities," taking advantage of the occasions that come your way. Whenever you get a chance, take it. Not every moment is equally opportune.

It is not always handy to speak to people about the gospel. There are special moments when there are unusual openings to speak on these matters. These are the moments we must look for. This is what happens if we redeem the time. For us as believers in Christ to be alert to such moments, when there is an unusual opportunity for you to speak, it will be necessary to be intelligent. Believers will need to know what they want to do and why, and this means practical planning. I think a person can first maintain a good confession. If I am to speak for the Lord I must live like a believer in Christ. How will a real believer act in the average situation? He will be found at the church services, he will pray, and he will read the Bible. He will be a supporter of the church work, ready to give his witness. He will be very careful where he goes and what he does. He will have an attitude that will show publicly that he is reverent toward God. He will be respectful toward authority, considerate of other people and charitable to the poor.

All these things taken together will speak of a certain consistency in manner and in conduct which is a great comfort to people who are going to turn to you to hear about the things of the Lord. A believer in Christ living in any community will be a peacemaker. For instance, it is not good common sense for a believer to have a number of hunting dogs in the backyard who yelp day and night and are an irritation to the neighborhood. It is not good for a believer in Christ to park his car in front of the neighbor's yard if that causes inconvenience to the neighbor. When he does these things he is not living wisely or maintaining consistent behavior.

The believer in Christ should be benevolent to all people; he should let his testimony shine forth. Paul says, "walk in wisdom": act with good common sense always. It is good common sense to act like one talks. The believer in Christ should look for the occasions when the neighbor he wants to reach would be particularly open to hear what he has to say. The believer can always be instant in prayer. He could have a prayer list of the people he wants to win and be ready to witness whenever there is an opportunity to do so.

All of this is part of living in wisdom. Today is the day. What can a believer in Christ do? He can walk in wisdom toward those who are without, buying up every opportunity.

SEASONED SPEECH
(Colossians 4:6)

Do you think it makes any difference how a believer in Christ talks to others?

> Let your speech be always with grace, seasoned with salt, that ye may know how ye ought to answer every man (Col. 4:6).

People notice those who profess to believe in Christ. Perhaps one reason for this is that the believer in Christ, by his affirmation of faith and by his claim to belong to the Lord Jesus Christ, actually has an advantage over the average man. As a believer in Christ he testifies that by the grace of God he is now a child of God. This is supposed to place him on a higher level than he was before. So, people sometimes look up to the believer with suspicion, as well as with envy, and perhaps with animosity.

The Lord Jesus told His disciples not to be surprised if the world hated them. The world hated Him first. That is the way it is even to this day. This latent hostility is manifested in the way in which the world is quick to criticize a Christian. One reason it is so important how a believer talks is that he does so much of it. For that reason he is much more susceptible and much more vulnerable. No doubt some believers fear lest their talk be considered pious. I always have a feeling of sympathy and a certain amount of impatience with believers who are afraid to talk like believers for fear people will think they are religious. Who is the person whose judgment counts? The individual who is a believer in Christ and knows the Lord, or the individual who is not a believer and knows not the Lord?

If I talk to a man and he does not talk about the Lord Jesus Christ because he does not believe in Him, that is natural and can be understood. But if I do not talk about the Lord Jesus Christ, is that natural? I believe in Him, then why don't I say so? The psalmist said, "Let the redeemed of the Lord say so" (Ps. 107:2). What we should be equally concerned about is that we avoid worldly conversation. It is one thing to be called pious because you refer to the Lord, but it is worse never to refer to the Lord and be worldly, even though nobody ever says anything about it.

The world would approve for the moment any views that

you express which are congenial to them. Whatever the subject may be, the world has some natural point of view about it. Something happens and the world will say, "This is by chance, it was bad luck or good luck." Or some work may be performed, and they will say, "This work is to the credit of certain persons; or the failure is to the discredit of certain persons." Life after death, they say is the influence a person leaves behind when he dies. They will say heaven is poetry. To them prayer is an intellectual exercise, and confidence in answers to prayer may actually be the sign of something wrong with the mind. The world may hear what the believer in Christ says, but they have their own explanation of those things. None of them honor the Lord because the world does not recognize the Lord.

On the contrary, God has His hand in everything that takes place. When work is accomplished, it is not to the credit of the individual who did it. If he had strength, it was given to him. If he had wisdom, it was given to him. If he is a failure, that is not to the total discredit of the man who was involved. The situation may have been such that he could not help it. The believer in Christ does not think that values are here and now; he thinks that moths and rust corrupt, and thieves break through and steal treasures laid up here. The believer lays up his treasures in heaven. Concerning life after death, the believer in Christ knows that to be absent from the body is to be present with the Lord. Heaven is a real place and God is there. Prayer is a function to be performed: "More things are wrought by prayer than this world dreams of." Confidence in answers to prayer is normal: believers expect them because they know God. This is the way it is with a believer in Christ.

If two were in conversation and the believer in Christ were to speak this way, he could be considered by the world to be saying impossible things. There could be the general judgment that he is putting on an act. This is a great snare to the Christian because it may cause him to keep quiet. Paul wrote: "Let your speech be always with grace, seasoned with salt, that ye may know how ye ought to answer every man." Speaking with grace will mean that the believer is concerned with the effect it has upon others. He will not say things impulsively. His speech will always be with restraint. He will be very careful not to exaggerate. He will not use questionable language.

Years ago, when I was lecturing in a college classroom, a matter came up in which a question was asked, and an answer that I had heard at a convention flashed into my mind. The man who had spoken it was a minister, but it was a slightly shady comment. Yet it seemed to fit into the situation. I took a chance and said it. I suspect I got what I looked for; namely, a big laugh from the class. But my heart hurt for three days. I had grieved the Holy Spirit within me. I should have been careful about any suggestive allusions in my speech, and I should have been careful to avoid inelegant phrases and uncouth expressions.

There are things other people can say that are not fitting to come from the mouth of a believer. His mouth is something that is used in communicating the gospel. So we should know how we are to answer any man. The believer in Christ should be very careful of his speech, that his public utterances be always with grace; thinking about doing people good in everything he says. He should remember this in conversation: "A soft answer turneth away wrath" (Prov. 15:1). He may also remember the Old Testament word that "a word fitly spoken is like apples of gold in pictures of silver" (Prov. 25:11).

THE IMPORTANCE OF FELLOWSHIP
(Colossians 4:7–9)

Do you feel that there is any value in knowing about the affairs of other believers?

> All my state shall Tychicus declare unto you, who is a beloved brother, and a faithful minister and fellow servant in the Lord: whom I have sent unto you for the same purpose, that he might know your estate, and comfort your hearts; with Onesimus, a faithful and beloved brother, who is one of you. They shall make known unto you all things which are done here (Col. 4:7–9).

It is not good for a man to be alone. This is true on every level. The woman who lives her spiritual life alone is limiting herself. The man who lives his spiritual life by himself is handicapping himself. We need fellowship; we need communion. It is a real comfort to have fellowship with someone else in the community; someone with whom to share. We can share with other people of like mind the situations we face, and this is good for us. If you want to grow as a believer in Christ, part of your growing must be the result of fellowship with other believers.

Let us see how Paul deals with this in verses 7 to 9. I suspect that oftentimes we pass these verses over rather lightly or we read them in a cursory manner, almost as if they were personal remarks made by Paul as he closes the letter. There is in these verses a real truth for us to grasp. We should keep in mind that Paul was being led by the Holy Spirit to minister to these people about their spiritual life.

We understand that Paul emphasized the fact that everything we have is from the Lord. We understand that we are complete in Christ, and He is high above everything. Believers have quick and ready access to Him by faith because of the promises He has given and the way in which He died for them. Yet it is also true that, while believers live in this world, they need faith, and faith can be nurtured; faith grows stronger in company with other people. This is shown forth in these verses, "All my state [my condition, my circumstances] shall Tychicus declare unto you, who is a beloved brother, and a faithful minister and fellow servant in the Lord: whom I have sent unto you for the same purpose, that he might know your estate, and comfort your hearts; with Onesimus, a faithful and beloved brother, who is one of you. They shall make known unto you all things which are done here." These fellow ministers were to comfort their hearts by making known to them how it was going with Paul.

When believing people get together and tell how it goes with them, that is helpful. It is meaningful to have a believing friend you can meet with to talk over how things are going, or if you are a housewife and you tell some other housewife how the Lord has helped and comforted you. Paul said, "All my state shall Tychicus declare unto you." Then he continued, "Whom I have sent unto you for the same purpose, that he might know your estate, and comfort your hearts." There are several things we can learn here. As I mentioned earlier, on the surface this sounds like a little note of personal chit-chat, but actually there is a profound truth here. True believers are generally scarce and they are often quite alone. Therefore, it is important that they, like Tychicus and Onesimus, find strength and comfort in communion and in fellowship with other believers of like mind.

MISERY LIKES COMPANY
(Colossians 4:10–11)

Do you realize the comfort and strength we get through fellowship with others who are going through the same things we are?

> Aristarchus my fellow prisoner saluteth you, and Marcus, sister's son to Barnabas, (touching whom ye received commandments: if he come unto you, receive him;) And Jesus, which is called Justus, who are of the circumcision. These only are my fellow workers unto the kingdom of God, which have been a comfort unto me (Col. 4:10–11).

I trust you are beginning to understand what Paul had in mind when he wrote to the believers in Christ at Colossae. At the beginning he pointed out that everything that matters is in Christ, and then he stressed "Christ is in you." Paul emphasized that we are complete in Him.

Some years ago the whole western world was inspired during World War II by the story of the four chaplains who gave up their places in the lifeboats of a sinking troopship to allow four others to escape drowning. The report told how these four servants of Christ stood linked arm in arm as their ship plunged into the depths of the ocean. I have often been filled with joy to realize the comfort they were to each other in that tragic hour, and I am reminded of the comfort we receive even now when we have fellowship with others in circumstances like ours.

These verses contain this very idea, and the particular line that strikes my heart is "which have been a comfort to me." Aristarchus, Marcus and Justus were three other servants of God who had fellowship with the apostle Paul, and who stood by him in his various troubles. Paul had strong reason to be comforted by them because they stood so close to him through all that went on. "My fellow prisoner saluteth you." The apostle himself was in bondage and here was another who shared with him. "And Marcus, sister's son to Barnabas." Then in parentheses "touching whom ye received commandments: if he come unto you, receive him" meaning to say, "concerning whom we have written you; you be ready when he comes your way to receive him." It is interesting that Marcus apparently belonged in the company because he was a nephew of Barnabas; he was one who was a comfort to Paul.

The person "Jesus, which is called Justus" (this is one of the places in the New Testament where we are made mindful of the fact that the name Jesus was a common name) was one of the three mentioned. Of all three it was said, "who are of the circumcision." For many, that word would almost pass them by. What is meant here is that they were Jews. Paul was a Jew but didn't do his work among Jews. Remember the New Testament record: it was Peter who went to the Jews and Paul who went to the Gentiles. Paul was known as the apostle to the Gentiles, and he magnified his office in connection with the work he was able to do with them. Here we find him writing to the Colossians who were Greeks, and he refers to three ministers, fellow servants, who were a real comfort to him. This says something for Paul: he was not committed to any one group. As we would say, he was not committed to delineations. He worked among the Gentiles, but if a Jew came along who was a good workman, he could join Paul. It also says something for those three men. We see something here that is strong: these men were of the circumcision. "These only are my fellow workers unto the kingdom of God."

Now let us look at the phrase, "unto the kingdom of God." How would they be workers unto the kingdom of God, and what is meant by "the kingdom of God"? The kingdom of God evidently refers to a relationship that exists between believers on earth and God the Father in heaven, which is accomplished through the Lord Jesus Christ, who is the King. The individual believer is yielded to Him, letting the Lord Jesus have His way in him, and he is thereby in the kingdom of God. Paul has here referred to the fact that these three workmen were his only fellow workers unto the kingdom of God.

Paul says in Romans there are at least three characteristics of being in the kingdom of God: righteousness, peace, and joy (Rom. 14:17). These fellow workers tried to get people to understand how righteousness is to be obtained through Calvary, when Christ Jesus died and we are declared righteous before God. Peace comes through the grace of God, and joy is to be had through the Holy Spirit.

These men, then, worked with the apostle Paul to preach this truth and persuade people about Calvary, about the coming of the Holy Spirit, and about the grace of God. "Which have been a comfort unto me." In all the discussions and arguments with the people who thought there were other ways of doing the will of God than just believing in the Lord Jesus Christ, these three Jews stood by Paul against the other Jews. They were a comfort to him.

It is a comfort and a strength to be endorsed when you are in any kind of controversy. If you could be endorsed by Jews when you had an argument with Jews, it would be comforting to you. Paul personally appreciated these faithful men who were dedicated to the Lord in their service.

THE MINISTRY OF PRAYER
(Colossians 4:12–13)

Have you realized that praying for spiritual growth in other people can be a ministry?

> Epaphras, who is one of you, a servant of Christ, saluteth you, always laboring fervently for you in prayers, that ye may stand perfect and complete in all the will of God. For I bear him record, that he hath a great zeal for you, and them that are in Laodicea, and them in Hierapolis (Col. 4:12–13).

This is the way the apostle Paul reports concerning one of his fellow servants, Epaphras, "Always laboring fervently for you in prayers, that ye may stand perfect and complete in all the will of God." Men who devote themselves to the preaching of the Word of God help Christians to grow in the Lord. The soul of any person is fed by the Scriptures and strengthened by the witness and testimony of other believers, but there is a function that is performed by ministers that is very important. God has arranged for some persons to care for the souls of others. The soul is nourished in faith by the Scriptures. Actually, faith comes by hearing and hearing by the Word of God, and the human soul can read and study the Scriptures to secure this faith.

This power of the Scriptures is operative only as the believer in Christ actually believes. Oftentimes he can do better when he has some other believer to take along as a guide and as a pattern. There is an aspect in which intercessory prayer on behalf of the reader or the listener matters. If you know somebody who is reading his Bible to understand about the gospel, that is wonderful. You should pray that he will understand what he reads. And if you learn that some person has started going to church, that is wonderful, but you should also pray for him. Pray that the pastor will preach the message he needs, and pray that his heart and spirit may be open to receive the message.

In verses 12 and 13 we have a description of the young man, Epaphras, whose home was in Colossae. This young man took seriously his responsibility and function as the minister in prayer. You remember in the book of Acts when deacons were appointed, the apostles said to the people, "We will give ourselves continually to prayer, and to the ministry of the word" (Acts 6:4), as if it was an actual task to be performed. Paul says, "Epaphras, who is one of you" because his home was in Colossae. It does not tell us he was a good or a clever servant; those attributes are not primarily important. The important thing is that he was a servant of Christ: committed to Him. A servant of Christ who "saluteth you." He sent them a greeting. "Always laboring fervently for you in prayers, that ye may stand perfect and complete in all the will of God. For I bear him record, that he hath a great zeal for you, and them that are in Laodicea, and them in Hierapolis."

These are the words that are spoken of this young servant of Christ called Epaphras. "Laboring fervently for you in prayers." The fact that this is expressed in the plural means he prayed more than one time. Perhaps he prayed three times a day, alone. Maybe he did it whenever he had opportunity with other people. In any case, it is said that he labored fervently for these Colossian believers, that they might "stand perfect and complete in all the will of God." They were to be mature and complete, with nothing left out. Epaphras prayed that they would take Christ as their Savior from sin and continue to confess their sins to Him. As Jesus was accepted as their Lord they would be brought into fellowship with Him.

Notice the next verse, "For I bear him record, that he hath a great zeal for you, and them that are in Laodicea, and them in Hierapolis." Having a great zeal for them was very earnest, very sincere. When Epaphras prayed for them he would pray earnestly, discussing before God the things he knew about them, and pleading for God's forgiveness and blessing upon them.

Evidently this church in Laodicea was a church close to the Colossian church. Paul wanted them to know Epaphras was praying for Colossian believers and for those at Laodicea and in Hierapolis. We have never heard about those, but they were another congregation. These three congregations were particularly significant to Epaphras, and he remained faithful in prayer as he ministered to these people before the Lord: that they might know the will of God.

When we look around we may have the feeling that there are troubles and circumstances in some churches that are not desirable. People may not be following as closely as they might, and may not be as obedient as they should be. When we are not able to do anything else, we can pray for them. Each of us should have in mind that we should pray for others that they might grow in grace and knowledge, so that their strength might be increased by the grace of God.

THE CHURCH
(Colossians 4:14–15)

Did you know that whenever several believers in Christ gather to worship God and to have fellowship with each other, this is the church?

> Luke, the beloved physician, and Demas, greet you. Salute the brethren which are in Laodicea, and Nymphas, and the church which is in his house (Col. 4:14–15).

The word "church" is a New Testament word, and the idea of the church is mostly a New Testament idea. There are those who recognize that what they now mean by "the church" can be seen in the Old Testament, and they refer to it that way; but the word generally was taken from New Testament language. It is a strange reality that there are no natural figures to illustrate what is meant by the church. Here the principal idea seems to be to speak of the church as the body of Christ. There are several different ways in which this idea has been set forth in the New Testament.

Always, of course, "the church" refers to believers in the Lord Jesus Christ. The Lord Jesus, in speaking of His believers, used the figure of the vine and the branches. He was the Vine and they were the branches. There are many branches but there is just one Vine. The unity, of course, was in Christ. Another figure that is used over and over again is the church as the temple of God. Here again, it is not so much the church as it is the group of Christians who are in mind. Still, that is what is meant in speaking of it as the temple of God.

Here the emphasis is upon the indwelling presence of Christ; just like God is in His temple, so Christ would be in the church. The church is also spoken of as the body of Christ. Whenever the word "body" is used, the idea is that of relationship between the believer as a member and Christ as the Head. As members of one body are related to another, so the members in Christ are related to one another. We speak of the church as the bride of Christ and here the emphasis is upon devotion, in love to God.

In our day we hear a great deal about the church in much of the teaching and literature that undertakes to interpret spiritual experience for us. It should be remembered that in the New Testament the church is pictured in fellowship or in communion; in fruitbearing or in love, but none speak of the church as serving the Lord. The individual believer serves the Lord, but the group as a whole seems to refer mainly to these other figures.

When we speak of the church as the temple of God, the body of Christ, or as the bride of Christ, we use that word "church" to mean all believers. But in this passage "Salute the brethren which are in Laodicea, and Nymphas, and the church which is in his house," we speak of the word "church" in a local sense, the church that is in his house. This comes close to the way we speak of our churches today. We refer to a church that has a name and represents a specific group of people who belong to that one particular congregation, just the way one would use the word "congregation." In this way we can think of churches in the plural, and that word is used in that way in the book of Revelation. There in chapters 2 and 3 we have the seven churches that are in Asia. I have made these comments with reference to the church because it is good for us to remember that when it is used in the New Testament the reference is to the believers in the Lord Jesus Christ, thinking of them together in a group. "Luke, the beloved physician, and Demas, greet you." Luke is commonly thought to be the author of the Gospel of Luke and of the book of Acts. He is referred to as the "beloved physician." He must have been close to the people and a very fine person to be referred to in this fashion. Demas stands alone, and this is of great interest to us. There is no comment at all here, and when we read in 2 Timothy 4:10, "For Demas hath forsaken me, having loved this present world," it is likely Demas' enthusiasm had cooled or he had become alienated from Paul. Apparently here is a man who had been one of the ministers with the apostle but who now had become interested in the affairs of the world.

The Lord Jesus said, "he that gathereth not with me scattereth" (Matt. 12:30), and this is what we have here. Paul named one man after another of a large company who worked together, seeking to further the gospel and Demas had been associated with them. But Demas loved this present world and did not want to continue. I suspect that when the apostle Paul emphasized "Christ in you, the hope of glory," he would stress that the things of this world would have to fade away, and in dealings with people he would not spend time talking about this world. Paul tried to get men ready to face God, and this probably irked Demas.

We can have in mind that this would not mean Demas turned away from the gospel into nothing, into the dark. Remember, the gospel is surrounded by the people of the world, and wherever the Bible is taught there are people of the world who have their own amusements and fellowships. They have their own religion in their own way. And, so far as Demas is concerned, he might have turned away from these believers in Christ to another group that he felt possibly had a better way of living.

BENEDICTION AND SUMMARY
(Colossians 4:16–18)

Do you think it matters if a man starts out in the ministry and then quits?

> And when this epistle is read among you, cause that it be read also in the church of the Laodiceans; and that ye likewise read the epistle from Laodicea. And say to Archippus, Take heed to the ministry which thou hast received in the Lord, that thou fulfill it. The salutation by the hand of me Paul. Remember my bonds. Grace be with you. Amen (Col. 4:16–18).

The task of the believer in Christ, having an old nature interested in this world and a new nature interested in the things of God, is to put off the old and put on the new. This is what Paul has been writing about in this whole book.

There is much more in this book than we have been able to point out. I hope that in this study you have learned something about "Christ in you," and also, as a believer in Christ, about yielding to one another and rejoicing in everything.

"Take heed to the ministry which thou hast received in the Lord, that thou fulfill it." This ministry apparently refers to the activity that we commonly have in mind when we refer to people who preach and teach the gospel of the Lord Jesus Christ. Such a ministry is an opportunity to serve the Lord by the consent of others. Nobody can make himself a minister in this sense. Congregations allow you to preach to them; this is the kind of thing that is conferred upon you by the consent of other people. It was this way in the New Testament and even to this present time. Here Paul is admonishing them to take heed to their privileges in preaching and teaching the gospel.

The church as a whole has an interest in it and they usually test people who want to have this privilege. Here Paul refers to the ministry that Archippus had received in the Lord. You may wonder what it would be like if a man did fulfill his ministry, and I want to draw your attention to 2 Timothy 4:1–5 where we read how the apostle Paul asked Timothy to fulfill his ministry.

> I charge thee therefore before God, and the Lord Jesus Christ, who shall judge the quick and the dead at his appearing and his kingdom; preach the word; be instant in season, out of season; reprove, rebuke, exhort with all long-suffering and doctrine. For the time will come when they will not endure sound doctrine; but after their own lusts shall they heap to themselves teachers, having itching ears; and they shall turn away their ears from the truth, and shall be turned unto fables. But watch thou in all things, endure afflictions, do the work of an evangelist, make full proof of thy ministry (2 Tim. 4:1–5).

Taking advantage of the opportunities as they have been given to you is what it means to fulfill the ministry.

We read in verse 16, "And when this epistle is read among you, cause that it be read also in the church of the Laodiceans; and that ye likewise read the epistle from Laodicea." The custom evidently was for these pastoral letters written by the apostles to be read in one church and then taken to another church, and so passed around. It is not known whether there was a letter written to the Laodiceans or whether some other letter was to be passed over there. At any rate, they were to exchange letters and keep on reading them.

The blessing of the gospel all through this book of Colossians is for everybody in Christ Jesus. The important thing in receiving blessings from God is to have a personal relationship with Him. It is God's idea to produce in us a life that would be the life of God through the Lord Jesus Christ. Remember, while the Lord Jesus Christ was here He said, "My Father worketh hitherto, and I work" (John 5:17). And then He said, "The Son can do nothing of himself, but what he seeth the Father do: for what things soever he doeth, these also doeth the Son likewise" (John 5:19). And if His Spirit is in us, that is the disposition in us. We do nothing of ourselves: God works and we work. It is God who initiates the movement in us. We yield to Him as we understand the gospel and He offers to forgive us. When we are born again He puts His Holy Spirit into our hearts. The Holy Spirit prompts us to serve God. And in serving God we try to remember the Lord Jesus Christ at all times, because the way the Lord Jesus did is the way we are to do.

In the course of this epistle we found that the believer in Christ is in two worlds: this world and the world to come. He has two natures: the old nature (his human nature that he got from his parents) and the new nature which he got from God. In the old nature, the old man deals with what he hears, sees, tastes, smells and touches. But in the new creature, the new man which he has in Christ Jesus, is of the Spirit and is minded toward God. He is the child of his parents so far as this world is concerned, but he is the child of God so far as the other world and eternity are concerned. It will help us to remember that these two worlds exist at the same time. When you are born again you start living in the other world, and in the life of Christ; the eternal life of God is operative in you now. This is the source of your strength and encouragement.

I hope you have felt this as we have gone along. You yield yourself unto God, deny yourself in the flesh, and the Holy Spirit moves in you to prompt you to do the will of God. The key verse in this epistle is "Christ in you, the hope of glory" (Col. 1:27).